Real Witchcraft: An Introduction

REAL WITCHCRAFT:

AN INTRODUCTION

by

KATE WEST & DAVID WILLIAMS

REAL WITCHCRAFT:
An Introduction

by

Kate West and David Williams

First Published in England 1996, as
Born in Albion: The Re-Birth of the Craft

ISBN 1-872189-47-4

I-H-O Books © 2003
Essex House, Thame, England. OX9 3LS.

No part or parts may be reproduced by any means whatsoever without prior permission being sought and obtained in writing from the publishers. The right of D. Williams and K. West to be identified as authors of this work has been asserted by them in accordance with the Copyright, Designs and Patents Act 1988.

10 9 8 7 6 5 4 3 2

This Book is dedicated to all
those who uphold The Craft

CONTENTS

Introducing Witchcraft	9
History of Witchcraft	15
Modern Traditions	21
Wheel of the Year	25
Cycle of the Moon	35
The Goddess and the God	39
The Elements	51
Tools and Equipment	61
Circle Work	73
Raising Power	85
Rites and Rituals	89
Magic	103
Planetary Hours	109
The Witch Within	117
Pathworking and Meditation	123
Covens and Initiations	147

TABLES AND DIAGRAMS

Table of Elements	57
The Pentacle	82
Invoking & Banishing Pentacles	83
Planetary Influences	109
Table of Correspondences	111

ILLUSTRATIONS

Herne the Hunter	14
The Moon	34
Drawing Down the Moon	59
Summoning a Quarter	59
Once in the Month . . .	59
Invocation to the Moon	59
The Altar	60
The Great Rite	60
The Rite of Wine and Cakes	60
Scrying	60

INTRODUCING WITCHCRAFT

The purpose of this book is to provide a basic introduction to Witchcraft. It is intended to answer some of the questions which are asked by those who are simply enquiring, as well as those who think that this may be the path for them. It does not set out to be a definitive guide on 'how to be a Witch' as Witchcraft cannot be learned from books or from people, it must be experienced. As with all such books, this one reflects the experiences, beliefs and working methods of the authors. Throughout the book space has been provided for you to make your own notes and there are several exercises which can be used by those on their own or by groups.

The book is not intended to replace the many other valuable books currently available, but as an introduction to more detailed study. For example, whilst the history of the Craft is covered in outline, we would recommend would-be historians to avail themselves of some of the many titles currently available on the market. We have not included a bibliography or reading list as we prefer to recommend titles taking into account the individual's needs as well as the subject they are interested in.

Witchcraft, Wicca, the Craft, the Craft of the Wise are all terms used by modern Witches. Witchcraft today is a renewed version of the old religion with its roots based in the Palaeolithic worship of the Spirit of the Hunt and reverence for the Triple Goddess.

Today's Witches still use these archetypes as the basis of their religious beliefs. Beliefs which include reverence for the male and female forces in nature and understanding of those forces within ourselves. Witches do not worship (or even believe in) a devil or Satan, but rather, they believe in personal responsibility and in personal growth. If you do wrong, such as losing your temper, it is your responsibility. You cannot say "the devil made me do it"! or pass the blame on to someone else. Witches also believe that spirituality should be a part of life, not apart from life; you do not celebrate or perform ritual, then go away and forget all about it until the next time. The sacred space of the Witch is not a building, such as a Christian church, it is the Circle, which can be set up at any time or in any place.

The Wiccan Rede (law) states *"An' It Harm None, Do What Thou Will"*, that means no intentional harm to oneself, others, or to the environment. Witches also believe in threefold retribution; whatever good/positive you do is returned to you three times and the same applies to bad/negative.

Witches may be female or male. Male Witches are not called warlocks or wizards, or anything else out of popular fiction! Witches may work on their own, with their partner, or in a group, sometimes called a Coven. Group working has the advantage of being able to combine the energies raised, rather like putting several batteries together, to create greater power. Some groups are working groups only, others accept and train newcomers to the Craft.

The Craft is non-hierarchical, each Witch being his or her own Priest or Priestess. The group or Coven is presided over by the High Priestess and High Priest who, by nature of their experience, are there to advise and guide. There is no organised body of Witches, no reporting to a religious leader or head office.

Witches celebrate the seasonal festivals of Samhain (31 Oct.), Yule (21 Dec.), Imbolg (2 Feb.), Oestara (20 March), Beltane (1 May), Litha (21 June), Lammas (1 August) and The Autumn Equinox (21 Sept.). These are the eight Sabbats or festivals which together, form the Wheel of the Year. Many of these have their modern or Christian counter parts such as Halloween, Christmas, Mayday, Midsummer, Harvest Festival. The Wheel of the Year is also echoed in our day to day lives. At any time we may go through stages of new beginnings, of reaping the harvest of our efforts, or of putting away the outworn.

Witches also observe the cycle of the Moon; from new (Maiden) through full (Mother) to dark (Crone). Again, the cycle is related back to our everyday lives.

Witches perform rituals to celebrate the Wheel of the Year and the Cycle of the Moon. They also perform rituals at other times and for other purposes, such as healing. If, for example, a person wished for help in obtaining a job, a ritual might be performed to give them extra confidence for the interview. Such rituals may be elaborate or simple. They may involve a number of people or just one on his or her own. They may take place indoors or outside, during the day or the night. Witches may work skyclad (naked) or robed, or even in their everyday clothes.

The issue of whether to work skyclad or otherwise arouses different feelings for different people. During the Witchcraze the removal of clothes made great sense. In a time when you probably only had one, or possibly two if you were well off, sets of clothing you would be easily recognised by what you wore, naked bodies seen from a distance would be unidentifiable. In modern times we must remember that Gardner, the "father of modern Witchcraft", was a naturist long before he was a Witch.

Today, the reasons for and against working skyclad are many and it is up to each Coven or individual to decide. Here are some of the more frequently heard arguments:

> The removal of clothes is a great leveller, what we wear says a lot about our status, by choosing what we wear we can choose what we appear to be.
>
> By working skyclad we allow the energy raised to be more accessible.
>
> Having to take your clothes off in front of strangers demonstrates genuine interest and commitment.
>
> If you can raise power and work magic a layer of fabric shouldn't make a difference.
>
> Working skyclad attracts the wrong interest, the type of enquirer who wants to know if there are any models in the Coven and can he take photos?
>
> Working skyclad may put off the genuine enquirer who doesn't feel comfortable taking their clothes off in front of strangers.

Some training groups or Covens will work robed when non-initiates are in the circle and skyclad when only initiates are present. Needles to say, skyclad working only takes place when the group is reasonably certain of being unobserved, indoors or in an isolated/secluded outdoor setting.

Working skyclad should not be confused with a prurient interest in sex. Whilst sex is considered a natural, wholesome, and enjoyable part of life, it is also part of the union in a committed loving partnership, not something to be undertaken lightly. Within ritual, the union between man and woman is token or symbolic.

Witches also believe in respect for nature (i.e. not taking more than is needed and repaying for, or replacing that which is taken), personal responsibility, reincarnation (or continuance of the spirit), divination or scrying and the practice of magic (i.e. the ability to change people, things and events by force of will, this only being possible if the request is in tune with nature). They also practice herb lore and healing in many forms. They make much use of meditation and concentration techniques. The roles of the Witch include: healer, teacher, advisor, bard (story teller), designer, innovator, author, poet, musician, herbologist, cook, tailor and many more. Not every Witch will be able to do everything, but within a group most of these functions will be carried out by someone.

Witches also have their own Rites of Passage:

> *Naming* – a ritual of giving a name, this is similar to a christening. However, there is no commitment to any particular path, whether pagan, Witch or otherwise. Children are brought up to examine alternative beliefs so that they can make their own decision when of age.
>
> *Handfasting* – joining or marriage, which may also be legalised through a Registry Office.
>
> *Rite of Withdrawal* – at the death of a friend or loved one, this reflects the belief that the soul or spirit continues.

There are other Rites which reflect important stages in the life of a person. In all these Rites there is a very strong element of celebration.

Witches believe that there are many paths and that it is up to the individual to find their own. This means that they neither recruit nor do they condemn the beliefs of others. Within the Craft there are also many different paths; some may involve Celtic imagery, or Norse, or Egyptian, others may use nature spirits or even pure thought forms. Again, it is up to the individual to chose the path which is most suitable for them.

Most of the above topics will be expanded upon during the course of this book.

Herne the Hunter — painting by Robert McNeill

HISTORY OF WITCHCRAFT

The religion of Witches has its roots over 30,000 years ago in the Palaeolithic era. Our ancient ancestors revered and worshipped the Horned Spirit of the Hunt. In a time when there was no supermarket or corner store the success of the hunt was essential, the life of the tribe depended upon it. Cave paintings from this time show men with horns upon their head. These paintings were intended to ensure that the kill would be made and the tribe fed. By the bronze age Horns had become a symbol of godhead.

As man developed agriculture, the cycle of fertility, life and death also became essential to the success of the tribe. These people did not have the benefit of sex education, and to them, the reproductive cycle was a mystery. They noticed only that the female went through three distinct stages of life: youth (the Maiden), a series of pregnancies and births (the Mother), and, if she lived long enough, a stage of no pregnancies or births (the Crone). This latter stage was also typified by wisdom, unlike the men who went out to hunt, the mother would have stayed largely within the confines of the tribal area raising her children, tending the crops and the livestock. During this time the women would accumulate wisdom in the ways of their people, in medicine and healing. Hence we see the origins of the Triple Goddess; she is Maid, Mother and Crone (or Wise One). Linked with worship of the Triple Goddess is the Cycle of the Moon which echoes the monthly cycle of women: Maiden – New Moon, Mother – Full Moon, Crone – Dark of the Moon.

Worship of the Horned God and the Triple Goddess can be seen in pre-Christian cultures all around the world.

The first European records of persecution of these ancient religions date back to the 5th century BC, when the Romans were torturing spell-casters. In 128 BC the festival of Dionysus (Greek God of fertility) was outlawed. The Christians do not have a monopoly on religious intolerance, despite their outstanding reputation in the arena. What we have to remember is that, on the whole, any hierarchical religion will have a need for money to support its structure. Any new religion wishing to establish itself is faced with the same problem; how to suppress the old religion, preferably without alienating too many of its adherents, and hence losing funds. It's very hard to tithe or tax the dead.

Hence it became necessary for the Christian church to try subtle methods of conversion. The Pagan festivals were taken over; Yule became Christmas (despite the fact the Jesus was born in February), Oestara became Easter, and so on. The Horned God became the devil, and the Triple Goddess was watered down to become Mary, virgin and mother. During the process the Crone aspect became lost — it wouldn't do for women to be revered for wisdom in a male dominated religion. The old sites of worship were taken over and changed.

The conversion of Pagans or Heathens (terms meaning people of the heath, or country folk and applied to any non-Christian belief) did not take place overnight. Christianity became the religion of Rome around AD 400, in England AD 700, Germany AD 900 and did not become established in Scandinavia until AD 1200. As it reached the status of dominant religion in any country it also became big business with large financial interests and hence of importance to the crown.

PERSECUTION
The first laws against Witchcraft were passed in France and England in AD 829. At this time the penalty was not death but penance. Around AD 900 the Canon Episcopi was published. This work, at the time considered obligatory for good Christian practice, referred to the evils of women, worship of the devil and Witches Sabbats all in one document. In France in 1022 the first official execution for Witchcraft took place. The charges laid were the same as those placed earlier by the Syrians against the Jews, by the Romans against the Christians, and later used by Hitler against the Jews and Romanies; charges of orgies, the sacrifice and abuse of children, cannibalism. It would seem that there is little innovation in ways of removing competitive religious persuasions.

By the end of the 13th Century the Christian church propaganda machine was well under way; Witches were described as malevolent. The incentives to expose a Witch were quite strong; you could get rid of an unwanted wife, competitor or enemy. In 1252 the Papal Bull also legalised the seizure of property, and its sharing between church, state and accuser. The scene was now set for the start of the Witchcraze which swept Europe and America.

By 1450 fear of Witches and Witchcraft had been whipped up to a fever. There are records of 100,000 men, women and children being legally tortured and killed — if you include those who died under torture, those subsequently acquitted and those who suffered at the hands of the mob during the whole of the continuing history of the Craft then the true numbers will be considerably more (estimates vary considerably and some believe the number may be as high as 9 million). At this point it is worth mentioning the legal difference between England and the rest of Europe including Scotland. In England Witchcraft was a civil crime and the penalty was death by hanging, unless of course treason against the crown was involved. Treason against the crown included plotting to kill your husband, as he was considered the King's representative within the household. In Scotland and the rest of Europe Witchcraft was considered heresy against the church and the penalty was burning. Hence the much used term, the Burning Times. Also to be remembered are the legal requirements of the time; disbelief in Witchcraft was guilt, pleading innocent meant you were hiding your guilt and refusing salvation, no confession could be accepted without proof of torture. Effectively, once accused, you had no escape.

The height of the Witchcraze in England took place during the years 1560 to 1660. The Witchcraft Act was first passed by Henry VIII in 1542 and repealed in 1547. Incidentally, this was one of the accusations against Anne Boleyn when Henry wanted to marry the pregnant Jane Seymour. The act was reinstated in 1563 by Elizabeth I, after the discovery in St Anne's Field, London, of a manikin of Elizabeth stuck with pins, at around the time when she tired of the plotting of her cousin Mary.

Progressive mis-translations of the Bible from the ancient Hebrew texts into Greek, Latin, German and English culminated in 1611 with the publication of the King James I version of Exodus 22:18 "Thou shalt not suffer a Witch to live". The craze peaked in the 1640s during the Civil War. Matthew Hopkins, failed lawyer and self styled Witchfinder General, was personally responsible for more hangings in 2 years than had taken place during the previous century. Hopkins and his assistants would descend on a town and commence a purge of Witches, charging a bounty on the head of each. Such was his reputation that the local authorities did not dare to offend him, lest they should suffer the same fate. The main charges levelled were those of hexing and cursing. In addition to relieving you of your unwanted wife or neighbour, you also gained a portion of their property, plus the certainty of a good reception in church. It was also convenient to be able to blame another for misfortunes such as failed crops and livestock, as you certainly couldn't blame the Christian God.

The last legal executions for Witchcraft took place in England in 1684, America 1692, Scotland 1727, France 1745 and Germany 1775. In England in 1736 the Witchcraft laws were repealed and replaced by prosecution for pretending magical powers. However, it didn't stop there. In 1751 a couple in Hertfordshire were killed by a lynch mob for the first time the mob leader was convicted. In 1951 the Fraudulent Mediums Act was passed replacing the previous act. In 1963 there was an attempt to reinstate the original Witchcraft Act, and again in 1982. There are still members of parliament today who would like to see the Act back on the Statute books. There are also good Christian folk whose actions can vary from anonymous leafleting to threats and actual physical violence. Thankfully these are in the minority, for the time being at least.

There are many in the modern Craft movement who feel that, with the increase in interest in Witchcraft and Paganism, there is a very real danger that a backlash will not be long in following. This will be partially the effect of disillusionment in "New Age" treatments and remedies sold by the unscrupulous for a fast profit. But one must also remember that the Christian church is a political and economic, as well as a religious organisation. Falling congregations mean falling funds and reduction in power, they will have to defend their position by whatever means are necessary. It is for this reason that some groups insist on secrecy, which should be adhered to. It is not only a question of respecting the wishes of the High Priestess and/or High Priest, it is for your own protection. It is worth noting that the Roman Catholic "Congregation for the Doctrine of the Faith" is simply a renamed section of the church. Its aims and intentions, tools and equipment, are unchanged. Most people are more familiar with its previous title: "the Office of the Inquisition".

THE MODERN REVIVAL
Whilst there are indications of a continuance of the Craft through the ages, most is conjecture and little is documented. The modern revival is largely credited to Gerald Gardner.

In 1889 Charles Leyland wrote 'Aradia, Gospel of the Witches' which he claimed he got from a Tuscany Witch. In 1921 Dr Margaret Murray wrote 'The Witchcult in Western Europe' from an anthropological viewpoint. Robert Graves wrote 'The White Goddess' in 1948. 'High Magic's Aid' was written by Gerald Gardner in 1949 as a work of fiction and under a pseudonym.

Gardner, born in 1884, claimed to have been initiated by Dorothy Clutterbuck, a New Forest Witch, in 1939. He also claimed that he was not allowed by Dorothy to publish a work of non-fiction until 1954 when he produced 'Witchcraft Today'. Witchcraft Today claimed to be the first work detailing the religion and rites of modern Witches. It can also be seen as a reduction of some of the rituals of the Golden Dawn to a more accessible level. In 1959, Gardner published 'The Meaning of Witchcraft', a book which contains information still of use today. Whilst Gardnerian and other traditions will be dealt with in more detail later it is worth noting one or two things about Gardner himself. Gerald Gardner had been a plantation manager and expert in medieval weaponry before his retirement. He was also a naturist and something of an eccentric. Gardner also founded the well known Witchcraft museum on the Isle of Man, forerunner of the Boscastle Witchhouse, both of which are now sadly closed.

Despite claims that Gardner invented modern Witchcraft, there's no doubt that worship of the Horned God and Triple Goddess has existed since pre-historic times. Although Gardner may have rewritten the 'Legend of the Goddess,' the 'Descent of Inanna' dates back to Sumerian times. Gardner may have been responsible with Valiente for the Charge of the Goddess as it is largely known today, but the Gnostic text 'The Thunder, Perfect Mind' contains strong similarities. Thus we are drawn to conclude that, although Gardner may be one of the first documented modern Witches, the historic pedigree of the Craft none the less exists. Actually it makes no difference whether Witchcraft as it is practised is old or new. Its validity lies in whether it works for the individual.

The next key individual in the revival was Alex Sanders. Alex was born in 1926 and allegedly initiated by his grandmother, although in an alternative version Alex claimed to have been initiated by Crowley. Alex was open about, and indeed notorious for, his involvement in the Craft. He believed that it should be accessible to any who expressed an interest and was interviewed, and often misrepresented, by all branches of the media. It is thanks to this that many, who otherwise would not have had access to the information, can now locate the individuals and books which enable them to have an informed opinion on the Craft.

Today information is available from many sources; most large book shops and libraries will have an occult or alternative religions section also there are advertisements in New Age magazines and shops. There are groups and organisations who can be located through such books and outlets.

MODERN TRADITIONS

There are many different traditions within the modern craft and it would be tedious, for the reader, to try to cover them all in depth. However, the main ones in England are; Gardnerian, Alexandrian, Hereditary, Traditional and Solitary. It should be noted that even within a tradition there will be differences from one group to another. One of the key points about the Craft is that there is always room for adaptation and growth.

GARDNERIAN
Gardnerian Witches are those who follow the traditions established by Gerald Gardner. They nearly always work skyclad and their rituals are usually followed quite strictly. Gardnerian ritual often includes use of the scourge.

ALEXANDRIAN
Alexandrian Witches follow the ideas and teachings of Alex Sanders. In Alexandrian Witchcraft there is a greater freedom within ritual, i.e. they will use systems outside of the mainframe of British or Celtic origins. They believe that "if it works use it" and intent being more important than simply "getting the words 'right' ". Alex himself said "if it's not nailed down — steal it"! Alexandrians may or may not work skyclad, this is usually a matter of personal or Coven choice.

HEREDITARY
Hereditary Witches claim that their rituals and Craft have been passed down through their families, either through blood line or marriage. They rarely, if ever, accept outsiders into their working groups.

TRADITIONAL
It is said that Traditional Witches claim that their workings pre-date the modern revival. This is obviously hard to verify. However,

it is true that there are some Traditional Witches whose knowledge of the Craft is as great as those who have studied and worked through the Coven system, but based on instinctive rather than acquired knowledge. The term Traditional is perhaps a misnomer. The term Instinctual is rather more meaningful and, as it leads to less confusion, will be used in this book. As it still remains a difficult concept to explain, the following account of one Instinctual Witch has been included to give perhaps a better feel to the term.

The story of one 'Instinctual' or 'Traditional' Witch.

> As a child, I grew up at a time when books and publications on Witchcraft were either fictional or sensational. My parents were fairly typical Christians i.e. they did their best and went to church two or three times a year. So Witchcraft was not "on the agenda" so to speak. However, even from my earliest day I knew I was a Witch. Sounds like a childhood fantasy, I know, but I knew it with the same inner certainty that I know I am alive. I followed the cycle of the Moon and was aware of its relevance to the female godform, the Goddess, and I acknowledged the Wheel of the Year through the seasonal changes. I was, and still am, in tune with nature and particularly good with animals, both domestic and wild. In my early teenage years I found I could influence people and events through an effort of will, now I know this to be the definition of magic. I was also psychically aware and could predict events, sense spirits and energies. Needless to say these topics were not discussed at home, but were actively discouraged.
>
> In the fullness of time, the Craft became more accessible so I was able to read of others and decided to try to seek out like minded people. It took a very long time before I discovered a working, training Coven. Here I was surprised that, despite the obvious

knowledge, experience and training ability of the High Priest, there was little understanding within the group members of the underlying principles of the craft. Things that came naturally to me, were foreign to them despite the years of training they had. It was at this time that I came across the concept of Sang Real or Witch Blood. The idea that a few people are born Witches, whether because of previous incarnations or hereditary bloodlines. This is not to say that the Craft is closed to those not of the blood, but rather that some people 'remember' the Craft whilst others are learning and experiencing it for the first time.

One of the most obvious differences between Traditional Witches and others is that many Traditionals do not allow metal of any kind into the circle — not even an Athame (see tools). Traditional Witches rarely follow a system of initiations, you either are or aren't! Many Traditionals work Solitary.

SOLITARY
Solitary is not a tradition as such, however, as they comprise a substantial proportion of Witches it is worth mentioning them as a separate category. Solitary Witches may follow one of the above paths or a variation, even one of their own devising. There are many reasons for working alone; it may be the difficulty of finding like-minded others to work with, family constraints (a Christian partner or parents!) or personal choice.

Solitary Witches may or may not use much ritual. Frequently the nature of their path means that much of their working is conducted with little noise or fuss. The ability to put up a working circle quickly and in silence extends the Solitary Witch's repertoire at an earlier stage than many Coven members who retain a tendency to hierarchical thought; leaving parts of a working to more experienced members through tradition, respect or nerves! A Solitary is more accustomed to adapting ritual to their own purpose simply because they do not have the additional effort of ensuring that others know what's happening. Nor does the Solitary need the agreement of anyone else to perform a particular ritual in a particular way. Having said that, the Solitary does not have the support of the rest of the group. If they have a bad day there's no one else to help set things up, raise power and clear away. The Solitary will need to rely on their own imagination and judgement to a far greater extent. Solitary working is not necessarily second best, and, whilst it can be a harder path, especially to start with, it is no less valid or rewarding.

Whatever your tradition, you will, from time to time, perform solitary rituals.

There are also groups who follow paths dedicated to specific Goddess and God forms: Celtic, Nordic, Teutonic, Dianic etc. This list is almost endless. There are groups who are female only, male only (rarely), homosexual. There are groups who accept and train newcomers, groups who don't, and some who will, but only a limited number.

There are, regrettably, also groups who misuse the Craft. The newcomer should steer well clear of any mention of the 'living altar', group sex or anyone who tries to part you from large sums of cash. Most groups have some kind of 'subs', but this is intended to cover costs, not to get rich quick. Some groups are very open and everyone knows there are Witches around, while others are highly secretive, not surprisingly given the history of the Craft.

Some confusion is often created by use of the term Pagan; it would be more accurate to refer to neo-Pagans. In fact there are no Pagans today — our Pagan ancestors were great believers in blood sacrifice, taking what you could (outside of the family or tribal unit), and violence. However, Paganism is a word which is used to cover a lot of the revived old religions. This includes Witches, Druids, Shamans and others. Whilst these have much in common, worship of a Goddess and a God and respect for nature for example, they are not one and the same. You can be a Pagan without being a Witch, and you can be a Witch without being a Pagan.

THE WHEEL OF THE YEAR

There are four major Sabbats: Samhain, Imbolg, Beltane, Lammas, and four minor Sabbats: the Summer and Winter solstices (longest and shortest days of the year), and the Spring and Autumn equinoxes (when day and night are equal). Originally, only the four major Sabbats were celebrated. Beltane and Samhain mark the light and dark halves of the year and reflect the two aspects of the God. Imbolg and Lammas come into play with the agricultural cycle; the times of spring births and autumn harvesting. The solstices and equinoxes can only have gained significance after the ability to measure, and predict with accuracy, the length of day and night throughout the year. Although there are dates given for the Sabbats, when most groups will celebrate, the solstices and equinoxes actually will fall on slightly different dates each year depending on the planetary movements. As the old pre-Gregorian calendar was twelve days behind ours, in medieval times Sabbats were celebrated on the eve of, rather than on the day. Most of the Sabbats are known by several names or the same names with different spelling or pronunciation, depending on the tradition which is being followed.

Originally the feasting for all of the Sabbats would have taken place over a three to five day period. This helps to explain why the Christians celebrate Christmas, for example, 3 days after Yule — when the Pagans would have had 3 days of feasting and would be a lot "tamer"! Interestingly enough Jesus was actually born in February, Christmas was moved back so that the celebration of the birth of the son would coincide with ongoing celebrations of the rebirth of the Sun. Most Sabbats have their modern or Christian equivalents and you do not have to look far to find local customs which reflect the origins of the feasts.

Samhain	31 Oct	Halloween or All Hallows Eve	
Yule	21 Dec.	Winter Solstice	Christmas
Imbolg	2 Feb.	Candlemas	
Oestara	20 March	Spring Equinox	Easter
Beltane	1 May	May Day	
Litha	21 June	Summer Solstice	Midsummer
Lammas	1 August		
Madron	21 Sept.	Autumn Equinox	Harvest Festival

SAMHAIN – 31 OCTOBER
(pronounced Sow-ain)

The start, and of course the end, of the Pagan year. In the Celtic Calendar it was an intercalary day, i.e. outside of the calendar. Originally this was a time of slaughter and feasting. At this time the people would assess their stores for the coming winter and decide which animals were unlikely to survive; these would be slaughtered so that the precious supplies of fodder would not be wasted. In some societies this would apply to people too, and those who were sacrificed went willingly, knowing this would help to ensure the survival of their loved ones.

Samhain is a time when the veil between the worlds is at its thinnest and those who have died may, if they choose, visit us again. For this reason lights were placed in the window to guide the loved ones home, and to deter any unwanted spirits; this is the origin of the Halloween lantern. Places were set at the feast for those who had gone, so that they too might join the celebration.

This is start of winter, the opening of the dark time of the year, with the Lord and Lady in their dark aspect.

At this time the Hunter comes into his role as Guardian of the Gates of Death. Herne the Hunter starts the Wild Hunt which continues throughout winter. Many groups will celebrate by enacting a Wild Hunt. The Spirit of the Hunt is invoked to pursue members along a predetermined trail through the woods. Should a person not complete the course by dawn, or should they turn back or get lost, then they are considered to have lost and have to pay a tribute to the Spirit of the Hunt.

Samhain is also known as the Feast of the Crone or the Death Goddess. The Crone is also the Keeper of Magic and Knowledge. She will pass knowledge on to those who can answer her riddles. For this reason Samhain is also a time of Scrying and Divination.

At Samhain the altar cloth is usually black and ritual will reflect the aspects of death and remembrance. One such makes use of two circles; one light and one dark, with group members passing from one to another, to remember their dead and the dead of the Witchcraze.

YULE — 21 DECEMBER

The Winter Solstice is the time of the shortest day and longest night. At this time the rebirth of the Sun is celebrated. The Oak King, Lord of Summer is born (although he will not take his place until Beltane). Celebrations and rituals are performed which remind us that in the depths of winter the Sun is reborn, and life is present even at the height of Death's power. Yule reminds us of the ever present cycle of life and death.

The Wild Hunt is at its most active, Herne rides the sky leading the souls of dead warriors. It was thought that any caught out on this night would be swept up and forced to join the Hunt, possibly never to return again.

At this time the Crone is preparing to shed her dark cloak for the white of the Maiden and spring.

Rituals at this time include altar cloth and decorations of red and green. Emphasis is on the rebirth of the Sun and on the presence of life in death. Often a Yule log will be produced with candles from each group member to represent the return of light.

IMBOLG – 2 FEBRUARY
Imbolg, Oimelc, Festival of Bridget or Bride

Imbolg literally means "in the belly". The first signs of returning life after the winter, are seen, the first lambs are born, the plants are in bud. It is a festival of returning life and rekindled fire. The Goddess is dominant and celebrated in her aspect of Maiden. The Great Rite is performed to honour the Goddess as life giver.

In ancient Rome the priests of Pan, the Luperci, would run naked, except for a goatskin girdle, through the streets, carrying a goatskin thong with which to strike people, especially women, to make them fertile.

It is also a time of year for personal housekeeping; to rid yourself of anything which is of no further use or which is holding you back. This is the origin of our Spring cleaning.

Ritual at this time will include the use of a white altar cloth. The emphasis is on the returning fire, the Sun and on the banishment of Winter.

OESTARA – 20 MARCH
Eostar, Oestre, the Spring Equinox

A time when the days and nights are equal, a time of balance.

Eostar or Oestre is the Northern European form of Ishtar of Astarte. Eostre was a Saxon Dawn Goddess and her symbols were the egg and the hare. The Christian version of this feast is Easter with it's Easter eggs and chocolate rabbits. The hare was changed for the rabbit, as Witches were thought to have the ability to shape-shift into the form of a hare.

At this time planting festivals were held to bless the seed for the coming season.

Festivals at this time celebrate the return of the Dying and Rising God: Attis, Mithras, Tammuz, Adonis and Osiris. To the Greeks it was the time of the return of Persephone from the underworld, a story which is echoed in the tale of the descent of Inanna (Sumerian Goddess). This is a time when the earth ends its period of mourning and new life is seen again.

Rituals at this time include a white altar cloth, for the Maiden, and revolve around symbols of returning life. There are frequently painted eggs and flower seeds to be given out to the participants. It is also usual to banish the unwanted and to welcome that which we wish to attain. Celebration is about welcoming the return of Spring.

BELTANE — MAY 1ST
Bealtaine, Walpurgisnacht

Named after Bel, the Celtic God of Light and Fire, Beltane is a festival of fire and fertility. Cattle would be driven between two fires, and the young men and women would jump over the flames, to ensure protection and fertility for the coming season. The people would re-light their own hearths from the Bel fire.

Maypole dancing was performed as part of the fertility rites, the pole being crowned by a circlet of flowers which would slowly descend as the ribbons wound tightly around the pole.

At this time the young would wear green to signal their sexual availability and it was traditional for them to pair off and enter the woods for the night. Any child conceived on this night would be considered the child of the God. Throughout its life, it and its mother would be cared for accordingly. Needless to say in times of uncertain food supply this was a great incentive to conceive on Beltane night. In some areas, the excuse for the night in the woods would be to collect May flowers. Hence it was considered unlucky to have May flowers in the house on May day — it signalled an unsuccessful night in the woods!

The more ancient form of celebrating Beltane involved the selection of a Stag Lord at birth. When he was fourteen, he would run with the deer. At some point the great stag would scent and confront the intruder. If the young man triumphed, he returned and mated with the maiden. This union between the two, trained from birth, to accept their fate or Wyrd, was the Great Rite, and it was performed for the fertility of the land and the people.

Beltane is the celebration of the marriage of the Goddess and the God. The May Queen is the representative of the Goddess and she chooses the May King to be her partner. In early ballads Marian and Robin Hood took these roles. The Goddess comes into her aspect of Mother and Queen. The Sun King comes down to reign beside his Queen. The Holly King of Winter falls to the Oak King of Summer.

Ritual at this time always includes the Great Rite with the Priestess and Priest representing the Goddess and the God. It is performed symbolically, so that the wine thus blessed may be shared by the group. Altar decorations are of red for the Goddess as Mother and Green for the God. Emphasis is placed on the celebration of fertility. Fertility in this context not being limited to pregnancy, but including growth of all kinds.

LITHA — 21 JUNE
The Summer Solstice, Midsummer

The longest day of the year, when the Sun is at the height of its power. Like Samhain, Litha is a time when the boundaries between the worlds are thin, but in this case experiences are more likely to be of a humorous nature.

Litha is a time of paradox; the greatest lies in the fact that even as the Sun is at the height of its power it starts to decline. The start of the Sun's decline is also marked by the birth of the Holly King the spirit of Winter.

Many groups, at this time, will enact the battle of the Holly and Oak Kings, although the Holly King will not come into power until Lammas. Altar decorations will be mostly gold and green.

LAMMAS — 1 AUGUST
Lughnasadh

The festival of Lugh the Celtic Sun God. This is Lugh's wake, although in earlier traditions it was deemed to be his wedding. He has been betrayed by his wife and slain by her lover. However, Lugh did not die, he was transformed into an eagle and later restored by his uncle Gwydion.

Lammas is the festival of the first of the harvest. Sacrifice is made to the land to repay it for the crops which are about to be gathered.

In some areas a volunteer was selected as King for the day or Fool. For one day, he would be entitled to the best of everything, and to anything he wanted. At the end of the day, he would be slain and his blood poured onto the land. This is enacted now by the slaying of the Corn King (a 'doll' made from corn).

There are many local customs associated with this festival including the making of corn dolls, and the eating of the sacrificial victim, in the form of bread, or ginger bread men.

At this time the Oak King dies and the Autumn commences. The theme of this Sabbat is the death of the God. However, it is also a celebration of the continuing cycle, in that the God will return again. Ritual at this time reflects this theme. We give thanks for what we have harvested in our personal lives, and consider whether we have sacrificed enough to pay for the harvest.

MADRON — 21 SEPTEMBER
Modron, the Autumn Equinox

This is the time of the completion of the harvest, harvest home, and the beginning of preparations for winter. In agricultural areas this is a time of rest after labours. As with the Spring Equinox, this is a time when day and night are equal. It is a time of balance, and of setting things right, paying old debts. It is the feast of the healer and the bringer of justice, the time of release of the prisoner. Things must be set back into balance before the winter or nothing will survive.

Ritual at this time reflects the celebration of the completed harvest and welcomes the storms of autumn which heal and replenish the earth. It also reflects the balance required in our personal lives. A time to discard old problems and outworn feelings, and to take on new aims and attitudes.

Ritual at this time will celebrate the successful harvest, but will also emphasise the need for balance in our lives.

The eight Sabbats taken together form the Wheel of the Year. This cycle is reflected in the sowing, growing and harvesting of the land. It is also reflected in our day to day lives. Each of us, in any affair, whether business or social, will have a time of sowing, growing, harvesting and laying to rest. The purpose of celebrating these festivals is to honour the earth as it goes through its cycle and to honour the Lord and Lady as they pass through their different aspects. But, equally important, it is also to help us mark and understand the way we pass through the same changes. It is no use to simply mark the feasts without understanding their deeper and more personal meaning.

The Wheel of the Year is actually a composite of overlaying beliefs. First we have the primitive belief; the appeasement of nature involving sacrifice, the world full of invisible spirits with which they lived. Worship was of the Moon and the Sun and powerful animals, such as the bear; here we have early Shamanistics beliefs and taboos relating to birth and to death. This was followed by the hunter gatherer cycle, the appeasement of nature through sympathetic magic, birth, death, rites of passage, fertility rituals. Then there came the agricultural cycle, blessing of the crops , harvest rituals, tribal and clan rituals. Certain elements link the three cycles: sacrifice, fertility and death. There was no organised religion and each group, family or clan, would worship in a prescribed way as set down by the elders, who gained knowledge from their ancestors. There was only verbal learning, as nothing was recorded and the ceremonies would be handed down by elaborate tales and stories involving myths, great feats of daring and pure fantasy. The Bardic tradition, of which only fragments remain in the old Folk songs and stories, is being revived nowadays. With the circle builders, between 3,200 to 2,200 BC there would seem to be a generalisation of art form relating to the building of circles over most of Europe, although there is no proof of an organised religion.

At the Sabbats it is not usual to seal the circle; this is not a time of magical working, it is a time of celebration and of feasting. Most rituals will end with the words "may the feasting begin", and then starts the party. Because of this many groups open their Sabbats to people who are interested in the Craft but who have not yet decided whether this path is right for them. These open Sabbats may also include those under 18, as the celebrations concerned can be tailored to reflect the age range of the gathering. In this way the Sabbat regains much of its original flavour, being a family and tribal or clan celebration of the season. Some groups celebrate the Sabbat in two parts; a closed formal ritual and an open family event. Typical examples include a fancy dress party with apple bobbing at Samhain, a beach picnic with a mock battle at Litha, a chocolate egg hunt at Eostar, Maypole dancing at Beltane. It is customary for regular attendees to assist by bringing some of the food and drink and taking part in producing the entertainment, this takes some of the strain off the hosts.

'The Moon' from the *Rider-Waite Tarot Deck*

THE CYCLE OF THE MOON

The Lunar (Moon) cycle is taken to run from the New Moon, waxing (increasing) to Full Moon, and waning (decreasing) through to Dark of the Moon, back to New Moon again. This cycle is generally considered to take twenty eight days. In fact the Lunar (or synodic) month takes an average of twenty nine days, twelve hours and forty four minutes. The time the Moon takes to circle the Earth takes twenty seven days, seven hours and forty three minutes, this is known as the Sidereal month. Confused? Well, the difference is caused by the fact that while the Moon orbits the Earth, the Earth is also continuing on its own orbit round the Sun and hence it takes the Moon an additional fifty-three or so hours to catch up. The Lunar Month is the one we notice, the one we see reflected in the sky. The Sidereal Month is used by astronomers and by those astrologers who demand accuracy in their calculations. This is why you cannot simply calculate the phases of the Moon for yourself, you need access to a reliable Moon calendar or Ephemeris. Our ancestors of course were not in a position to look the phases up in a diary or use the local library, they simply looked up into the night sky and saw the Moon as she was.

Worship of the Moon goes back to the earliest times, cavemen inscribed Lunar calendars on cave walls; some of these are roughly dated from 8,000 to 40,000 BC. The Babylonian Ishtar, the Sumerain Sadarnuna, Greek Selene, Roman Diana, Celtic Arianrhod, and many others were all worshipped as Goddess of the Moon. Legends and tales about the Moon also come from many countries, cultures and times. To the Australian Aborigines the waning Moon was a woman who partied too much, so that she lost weight and finally had to go away to rest. She was reborn each month and regained her strength before starting to party it away again. The American Indian Dacotahs believed that the Full Moon was nibbled away by mice until it was all gone, being reborn, growing and then sharing the same fate as its predecessor. This myth was shared by some of the Balkans (in Europe) except they told that the Moon was eaten by wolves. Not all cultures saw the Moon as female; Greenlanders tell the tale of Malina and her brother Aninga. Malina fled her brother, fearing incest, and she became the Sun; her brother pursuing her became the Moon. It is his incessant hunting of her which makes him become thin until he is forced to rest and recuperate. The Egyptians had male and female Moon deities, Khonsu and Thoth being Moon Gods and Bast and Utchait being Goddesses associated with the Moon.

Throughout history, right up until recent times, there have also been tales and stories connected with the Moon and its effects on people; moon-madness, Lycanthropy (werewolvism), suicide and murder. Although these tales are largely 'out of fashion' in these enlightened times there is a growing body of evidence that the Lunar phases do in fact have an effect on both the mind and the body of both women and men. Hardly surprising when you think what the pull of the Moon does to the tidal flow of oceans and seas and when you remember that our bodies are comprised mostly of water. There are scientific studies linking the phases of the Moon to crime rates, to reproductive cycles and to the function of the brain. It is possible to predict mental, physical and emotional, highs and lows by using the study of bio-rhythms (cyclical changes in these energy levels). These studies are used not only by individuals but also by large commercial organisations wishing to gain the best out of their executives. So the effects of the Moon are not just superstition but play a very real part in our day to day lives.

It is possible to have your own bio-rhythm chart produced, alternatively you can keep a diary of your own energy levels in order to discover how the Moon effects you. Of course women already have an obvious monthly cycle; however, men will also find they experience fluctuations which revolve around a lunar cycle. You can track your own physical, mental and emotional cycles and then predict which days are likely to be good for which activities. This is another step in self-knowledge which is important for anyone wishing to tune in to the natural side of their self and is essential for anyone wishing to work ritual or magic.

As you can see from the table below, the phases of the Moon are linked to the Triple Goddess and certain workings are best performed at certain times. The Full Moon, of course, is one of the key meeting times of the Witches, at this time the ritual of Drawing Down the Moon is performed. For three nights before the New Moon there is no Moon visible in the sky, this period being known as the Dark of the Moon; at this time no magical working should take place. There are thirteen full Moons each year, which together with the eight Sabbats, give us twenty-one Witch festivals per year.

SOME LUNAR CORRESPONDENCES			
Moon Phase	New	Full	Waning
Aspect	Maiden	Mother	Crone
Goddess	Persephone	Demeter	Hecate
Colour	White	Red	Black
Alternative	Yellow	Blue	Amethyst
Rites	Beginnings Growth	Celebratory Fruitfulness	Banishing Harvest

As with all such tables in this book, this is just a beginning. It is important that you develop your own correspondences, as these will be more appropriate and meaningful to you.

THE GODDESS AND THE GOD

Isis, Astarte, Diana, Hecate, Demeter, Kali, Inanna, Nepthys, Sekhmet, Melusine, Arianrhod, Cerridwen, the Lady and many other names.

Osiris, Anubis, Set, Herne, Cernunnos, Pan, Bacchus, Zeus, Apollo, Silvanus, Odin, Thor, the Lord and so on.

One of the things which seems to cause some confusion for newcomers to the Craft is the names of the Goddess and the God. Both have been worshipped by many peoples in many places and in many times, this is why there is such a plethora of names. Some individuals and groups will settle on one particular tradition (Celtic, Norse etc.) and relate to the Gods and Goddesses of that tradition. Others will use different traditions at different times, and yet others, will refer to the Lord and the Lady. Really, the main thing to remember is that you cannot mix and match within any one ritual. It is also not a good idea to experiment with the darker aspects until you know exactly what you are doing. These aspects are not bad in themselves but it can be very dangerous and bring about changes in you, which you do not intend. There are many such warnings in this book, which are placed here for your guidance and protection. Contrary to popular belief, it's not a rather transparent method of trying to hide the deepest secrets! We know that there are those who will immediately rush out to try what has been recommended against. Fortunately the nature of the Craft is such that, if you ignore the fundamentals, it is only likely to rebound on yourself; at least you will not harm others.

Obviously, if you are within a group, you must work within their system; it's no use having six people in a circle working in the Celtic tradition and the seventh invoking Thor! However, when working on your own, use whatever you feel most comfortable with.

The Goddess, as we have already said, is worshipped in her three aspects of Maiden, Mother and Crone. These link directly to the phases of the Moon and to the Wheel of the Year. These three aspects also have relevance in our lives. Not just as part of the ageing process, but also in our day to day life. All things have a cycle of growth, maturity and decline. It is a useful exercise to look around and notice these stages all around us, as well as within us.

The God is worshipped in two aspects: light and dark, summer and winter, the Oak King and the Holly King. Again this is reflected in the Wheel of the Year and in our daily lives.

One of the key parts of the Craft is the need to identify, accept and integrate all the aspects of ourselves, including the darker ones. Unless we are whole, we cannot function fully. We also need to integrate the male and female aspects of our personalities; you cannot work with just the Gods or the Goddesses. For these reasons, time spent studying the legends and tales, and reflecting on their relevance in our lives, is essential. Knowledge of at least one tale is often a requirement in order to join a Coven, or for 1st degree initiation. An outline and commentary on some of the tales is included at the end of this chapter.

So how do we work towards understanding the God and the Goddess and integrating all the parts of ourselves? Well, it isn't easy. The path to self knowledge is long and difficult, and is covered in the chapter entitled 'The Witch Within'. However, in addition to reading and reflecting on the legends, other techniques frequently used are: meditation, dream analysis, and pathworking. As an example of the latter, a Pathworking or guided meditation to meet the Goddess is included below.

The purpose of a Pathworking is to allow individuals access to their subconscious. It takes the form of a story told which the participants follow. At one or more points the individuals will be told to ask a question or make a choice. These times are indicated in the following by the word (pause . . .); other instructions to the reader are also in brackets. It is not hypnosis and persons taking part do not lose control of their thoughts or actions, although occasionally you do find someone who relaxes sufficiently to fall asleep! As with all such Pathworkings it is better if one person can read this aloud to a group, that person should have a clear but calming voice and, whilst not being monotonous, should avoid dramatic 'ups and downs'. The reader is then in a position to observe those taking the meditation, and if necessary they can 'wake' anyone who seems to be experiencing something they do not like. Should it be necessary to wake someone, the best way to do this is to gently touch them on the arm, call them by their name and ensure that the first thing they see is a reassuring smiling face. Note that there are no subliminal or 'post hypnotic' suggestions included, this would be trespassing into the realms of psychotherapy and is best left to the experts. At the end of the Pathworking discussion of people's experiences should be encouraged. However, respect the wishes of those who do not wish to share their experience with the group. Where they have one, participants should write up their experience in their Book of Shadows.

PATHWORKING TO MEET THE TRIPLE GODDESS
(Before starting make sure the room is warm enough and that the chance of interruptions and distractions is minimised, turn off the phone, put the cat out, for example.)

"We are going to do a Pathworking to meet the Triple Goddess. Please follow the story and resist the temptation to stray from the path. During the story you will be allowed to ask a question, and hear an answer; please do this 'in your head' not out aloud. If you find that you are not able to relax sufficiently simply listen to the story; you may find that you benefit from the experience at a later date, in your dreams perhaps. If you have any difficulty please remain where you are and raise your hand — I will then come to you. Is everyone comfortable?

(Take time to ensure everyone is comfortable, warm enough, does not need the bathroom etc.)

Sit comfortably, uncross your arms and your legs. Relax your hands in your lap. Close your eyes.

Let your body relax. Feel the weight of your body resting and relaxing. Relax each part of your body; relax your toes and feet, relax your calves and thighs, relax your hips and tummy, relax your back and chest, relax your neck and shoulders, relax your arms and hands, relax your face and head.

Listen and follow the sound of my voice, all external sounds and distractions fade away and you hear only the sound of my voice. Know that, if at any time, you experience anything you do not like, you will be able to open your eyes and you will be alert and ready to deal with anything you may need to.

Relax your breathing, breath in through your nose and breath out through your mouth, breath in to the count of four, hold your breath to the count of four, breath out to the count of four. Breath in through your mouth and out through your nose.

You are walking through the forest at night. The night air is warm and a gentle breeze rustles the trees. The birds are singing their night song. The trees around you seem welcoming and friendly. Around you, you hear the sounds of small animals making their way homewards for the night. Underfoot the grass is soft and springy. The fragrance of the night flowers is relaxing and soothing. You sense a feeling of peace and safety as the forest settles down for the night. You feel content and secure, knowing you are on your own, but not lonely, and nothing can harm you.

As you walk through the forest you can see the sky above you darkening to a deep rich midnight blue. The stars seem nearer and brighter than usual. You walk on, enjoying the warm night air and the peace and solitude of the woods. Gradually the trees thin and you find yourself walking towards a clearing. There is a large grassy glade opening in front of you and the land slopes gently towards the centre where there is a broad deep pool.

On the other side of the water you can see the open space continues up to the forest's edge again. The trees on the other side appear dark and impenetrable. You walk slowly down the slope towards the waters edge. The air is warm and still, although the trees behind you still move a little in a high breeze. The night sounds are growing quieter. You feel serene and secure. You reach the edge of the water and gaze into it. The water is still and dark and immeasurably deep. Not a ripple disturbs the surface.

Here, you can see the reflection of the moon above. The moon is full and bright and bathes the clearing in warm silver light. You stand still and relaxed at the water's edge. You feel a sense of expectation, as though what will happen this night is very important.

As you watch the reflection of the moon in the water you become aware of three figures standing on the opposite shore.

The first is a beautiful young maiden, dressed in a flowing, shining white dress. Her hair is pale golden and hangs loose over her shoulders. It is braided with flowers that resemble the stars in the night sky. Her smile speaks of youth and laughter.

The second figure is a mature woman dressed in a long crimson robe. Her hair is a warm rich brown. She carries a basket of the fruits of summer. Her face is kind and maternal and she smiles in a warm and comforting way at you.

The last figure is older. Her dress is all of black and her hair is covered by a black veil. The smile on her lined face speaks of wisdom and understanding. Although she is past her youth her beauty is of a deep and enduring quality.

The figures stand still and motionless. Although they are strange to you, you feel no fear or apprehension. Their presence fills you with a feeling of calm and security. As you look at them the expanse of the water seems to shrink and you feel as though you could reach out and touch the three women. As you watch one of the figures steps forward and holding out her arms to you, bids you welcome. She tells you that you may ask one question. Stepping to the very edge of the water you reach out your hands and take hers and you ask your question. (pause . . .)

Remain in silence and listen for her answer (pause . . .)

When you have received your answer, she smiles and releases your hands and you both step back. The distance across the water returns to its former expanse. The three figures smile farewell at you and you turn and retrace your steps.

You walk back up the grassy slope away from the moonlit pool. Just before you enter the forest again you turn, but the three figures have gone. Once again you become aware of the night sounds of the forest, you become aware of the soft ground beneath your feet and of the warm night air. As you walk on you think on the words of the woman at the pool. You will remember those words and this night, as you know the meaning will become clearer to you with time.

You retrace your steps through the trees. Taking your time to enjoy the peace and tranquillity of the woods. The silence is only broken by the rustle of the breeze in the treetops. The forest is still reassuring and friendly. The air is still warm around you although the breeze is perhaps a little cooler now.

The forest fades and once more you become aware of this room you are in, the floor beneath you, supporting your weight. The others around you. You may open your eyes when you are ready (pause . . .) (Wait until all or most have opened their eyes. This is the time to wake anyone who has fallen asleep.)

Clap your hands and stamp your feet to earth yourself."

(Where practical, participants should be given a hot drink or something to eat to help them to return fully to the here and now. But try to ensure that discussion of experiences does not take place whilst the reader is out of the room.)

Those who do not work within a group may find that the easiest way to make use of the Pathworking technique is to record the 'story' onto a cassette and then play it back to themselves at a suitable quiet time.

More details on guided meditation and pathworking, together with further pathworkings are included in the chapter entitled "Pathworking and Meditation".

Tales of the God and the Goddess abound from every culture, religion and part of the world; Greek, Roman, Sumerian, Babylonian, Egyptian, Celtic, Norse and so on. All the tales have something to tell us and a relevance to our lives today; they speak of human emotions and failings, as well as choices and difficulties. In times when reading and writing were the province of only a few, knowledge was passed on through the oral traditions. Simple facts were elaborated into memorable stories, which would catch the imagination of the listener. The lessons thus learned being concealed within a pleasing cover — a bit like a sugar coated pill. Today we are unused to looking deeply for truth and will all too often dismiss a story at its face value, hence losing the message within.

Below is a very brief outline of the story of the Descent of Inanna, demonstrating just one of the hidden messages concealed in the old legends. It would be profitable for the reader to take the time to look up the full version of the story, then, perhaps with greater understanding, to re-evaluate some of the other legends of the God and the Goddess.

THE DESCENT OF INANNA

The story of Inanna is first recorded in clay tablets dated around 3,000 BC, although there are indications that it existed previously as an oral tradition. The story of the Descent of Inanna is only a part of the full legend of Inanna and tells the tale of Inanna and her sister Ereskigal.

Inanna is the Sumerian Great Goddess of Love and War, Queen of Heaven and Earth, Holy Priestess of Heaven. Ereskigal, her sister, is the Queen of the Underworld. Together they represent the young and old, light and dark aspects of the Goddess. Their story epitomises the search for wholeness and integration of the conflicting aspects of the self. Inanna has no knowledge of the other side of Life and Love, which is the Never-ending Dance of Death and Rebirth.

Inanna travels to the Underworld to attend the funeral of her sister Ereskigal's husband, Gugulanna the Bull of Heaven. In order to enter the Underworld Inanna must leave one of her earthly and heavenly powers or attributes at each of the seven gates of the Underworld. Thus she is stripped of her titles, powers, jewellery and clothes for she can only face her darker self naked and bowed. (Seven is the number of wholeness and represents the seven classical planets and initiatory trials. This perhaps is the origin of the dance of the seven veils.)

On reaching the Underworld Inanna is seized by her sister and turned into a 'piece of rotting meat' — being divine she experiences death as decay and dissolution. For Inanna has failed to ask the Question of all Questions, the great Initiatory Question, which in this case can be phrased as "Sister what ails thee and what can I do to relieve thy suffering?"

Meanwhile, after she has been gone for more than three days, Inanna's faithful servant Nishubar, pleads to the Gods for Inanna's return. Enki, God of Wisdom is the only one who fully appreciates what the loss of Inanna means; the land is barren, there is no love, laughter, daring or poetry. Enki creates two creatures who empathise with Ereskigal in her grief. The creatures ease the pain of Ereskigal who offers them gifts, these they refuse, taking instead the body of Inanna reborn.

Inanna now wishes to leave the Underworld but no one may leave the Underworld unmarked, a part of her must stay there. She must find one to replace her. In this case it is her lover Dumuzi, who did not miss her during her absence. Thus her replacement is also someone who must learn compassion and empathy.

Inanna has taken a true initiatory journey, because she wants to Know and as such she Dares Wills and Surrenders to the process of Becoming, leaving behind who and all she thought she was. Why? Because she trusted more than anything else, who she could become? The Initiatory Question mentioned is, for us today "What can I give of myself?" rather than the more frequently asked "What will it do for (give to) me?"

Other similar legends:
Persephone, Greek Goddess of the Underworld, is kidnapped by the God of Death. Her mother Demeter, Goddess of the Earth, searches for her until the Gods lend their aid. As part of the return of Persephone it is necessary that she spend a third of each year in the Underworld. The third part of this triple Goddess is Hecate, Goddess of the Moon and the Crone.

Ishtar, Babylonian Moon Goddess descends to the Underworld to retrieve the body of her lover Tammuz. This legend goes on to finish with the moral: " Who denies sex denies life, who denies Death denies life. Such a one will find neither life joyful nor death easy." This can be applied to the Descent of Inanna in the terms "Who denies their dark side will not fully enjoy their light side".

Probably the most well known tales are those of the Egyptian Isis and Osiris, tales which are told in our schools today. But here modern practice has been to paint the characters as either good or bad, without acknowledging that there is both in each of us. Below is an outline of one of the versions of the legend.

ISIS AND OSIRIS
The ancient Egyptians believed that Ra, before he became Sun God, was ruler over all Egypt. He had four children: Isis, Osiris, Nepthys and Set. In this culture incest within royal lines was not a sin nor a crime, it was a necessary means of keeping pure the royal bloodline and ensuring continuity of a successful reign. Hence Isis was married to Osiris and Nepthys to Set.

Now Ra grew old but would not pass on his throne to one of his children. So Isis pondered how she might make her husband Pharaoh. Thoth, God of Wisdom, told her that only by knowing the secret name of Ra might Isis gain power over him. So Isis plotted and eventually tricked Ra into revealing his secret name and killed him. As a result Ra took his place in the heavens and Isis and Osiris came to be Pharaohs over Egypt.

Meantime, Nepthys was jealous of the good fortune of her sister Isis, not only because of the rulership of Egypt, but also because she, Nepthys, was unable to conceive a child by Set. So Nepthys disguised herself as Isis and became pregnant by Osiris, the child becoming the God Anubis.

Set, understandably, was not happy and plotted his revenge. He gathered together his friends and laid a great banquet for Osiris. At the height of the celebrations he produced a magnificent jewelled casket and said that who so ever fitted in the chest should keep it. Needless to say the casket fitted Osiris perfectly. Once Osiris was inside, Set threw shut the lid and sealed him inside. The casket was then cast into the Nile where it was carried away.

Isis distraught, searched Egypt for her husband-brother, finding him many years later within a tree which had grown around the sealed chest. Isis frees her husband and is in the process of reviving him when Set discovers what has happened. This time he is truly angry and hacks the body of Osiris into thirteen pieces, casting them hither and thither over all the lands.

Isis, grieving, now searches for the parts of her husband so that she might give him a proper burial. Remember that the Egyptians believed that your body must be whole in order to go on to the after life. Nepthys and Anubis join Isis in the search and together they find twelve of the thirteen pieces, the phallus being missing. With her magic and healing Nepthys fashions a new phallus from wood which subsequently impregnates Isis. The first example of artificial insemination? The twelve parts are then buried in separate sites, unknown to Set. Osiris then passes to the after life becoming King of the Dead and symbol of resurrection.

Here we have a tale of very human emotions; ambition, envy, jealousy, covetousness, lust and murder. Not quite what is more commonly told, that Isis and Osiris were 'good', Set 'bad' and Nepthys as the dark Goddess. We see Isis as devious, as well as the grieving wife, Osiris as an opportunist, as well as a good king, Set as victimised, as well as jealous and angry, and Nepthys as healer and barren woman, as well as deceiver and adulteress.

It is worth studying more of the tales of ancient Egypt as there are many other stories. For example: Nepthys was concerned for the child Anubis' safety: she worried that Set might harm the child that was not his. Therefore, she wove a basket and placed him inside, trusting the waters of the Nile to ensure his safety. The basket was washed up in some reeds (starting to sound familiar yet?) and Anubis raised in safety away from Set's anger. This story predates Christianity by some 3,000 years.

Once you start to read the old legends and compare them, you will notice an interesting thing; the same stories pop up in different places, times and under different names. But the basic lessons they teach us are as valid today as they were then.

WORSHIP

Worship, to a practitioner of the Craft, is an integral part of every day. It is not set apart as in other religions. Whilst the Sabbats and Esbats are times of worship, they are not the only times. Our place of worship is the Sacred Space, the circle, which is wherever we put it, not a fixed building. To understand this we must look at what worship actually is.

Every thought in the human brain, in its earliest state, is energy. Everything we do and every action we take begins with a conscious or subconscious thought. Objects we take for granted in the world around us all begin, and come from, a thought from those who created it. Tools, clothes, furniture, the houses we live in, the vehicles we drive, recipes we cook by and the pots we use to cook in, all originate from a thought, whether ours or the creator's.

Witches believe that thought is a powerful tool which can be used to create change. This thought is neutral until it is directed towards its destination or goal. Thought, therefore, is energy which once originated cannot be taken back or dispersed. You cannot unthink something. However, the human will is governed by personal choice. If you think you will do the washing up it doesn't mean it will happen unless you physically do it. Neutral thought is put in to gear by a person's actions, and thus it becomes manifest.

To think of a God or Goddess creates energy which travels towards its destination. In Witchcraft, worship can take place by thinking or doing any activity which brings the chosen God forms into the mind of a Witch. A walk in the British Museum looking at the displays of votive objects can be an act of personal worship. Should you be artistic and desire to create an image of your chosen God or Goddess form, this too is in its own right an act of worship. This is one of the reasons why Witches are encouraged to make their own tools and equipment. Many other things that we do in the normal day to day running of our lives can rightfully be called worship, as long as they are directed towards a God form. Another good way of worship is to dedicate a mundane task to your God form. Digging the garden, mowing the lawn, doing the weekly shopping, are very ordinary humdrum tasks. The energy used both mentally and physically can be directed towards a God or Goddess, and strange may it seem, by doing this it is quite possible to find the task becoming easier to fulfil. It is in this way that you can experience the Gods helping you in a very practical way.

THE ELEMENTS

The Elements are represented in the five points of the Pentacle. They are Earth, Air, Fire and Water, and Spirit (or Ether). All things are made up of these. Earth, Air, Fire and Water are represented on the altar, and are invoked when putting up a circle. This invocation is called summoning the quarters. Spirit is provided by the self. This is why it is important that your intent should be pure, and free from distractions.

Knowledge and understanding of the Elements is essential in order to work ritual and magic. This means knowing them in their tangible forms, such as earth as rocks, stones, sand and soil etc. It also means understanding their intangible forms; in us, Earth is our physical body, blood, flesh, bones etc.; Air, our thoughts, dreams and reflections; Fire, our passions, lust, anger etc.; Water, our emotions. It is useful for both newcomers to the Craft and experienced Witches to spend time examining and experiencing the Elements. It is by understanding the Elements that we learn to understand and hence control, those aspects of ourselves.

The Elements are also represented by Elemental kingdoms and Elementals. The Kingdoms are the realms of the Elements — places where each Element has dominion. Living within these Kingdoms are the Elementals, creatures made of that Element, who live entirely in and on that Element.

Air:	Sylphs, creatures who are made of air and live in the air.
Fire:	Salamanders, usually depicted in a lizard-like form they live in the flames.
Water:	Undines, creatures of and in the water.
Earth:	Gnomes, beings who live and work in the earth.

Using visualisation and pathworking techniques we can visit these places and meet with these beings; see the chapter on Pathworking and Guided Meditation. This helps us to understand the Elements within and without. A fuller way of experiencing the Elements is to devise a whole ritual around them. One is included at the end of this chapter; if you read through it you should see easily how to adapt it for any of the other three Elements, using the appropriate element Pathworking and altering the aspects to match each Element.

Each of the Elemental Kingdoms is guarded and ruled over by its own Guardian of the Watchtower, sometimes referred to as an Archangel. Archangels have dominion over the Elements and the Elementals. As you work with them you will begin to build up your own picture, which is more valid than one painted for you by someone else, this is why the outlines below have been deliberately kept to a minimum.

The Guardians are generally represented as:

AIR   RAPHAEL   SPRING
A beautiful adolescent, dressed in flowing yellow robes with lavender facings in a land of soft gentle breezes.

FIRE   MICHAEL   SUMMER
A stern young man, dressed in a velvety red tunic with emerald green facings in a warm tropical atmosphere, laden with the scent of exotic flowers.

WATER   GABRIEL   AUTUMN
A man in the prime of life with an amiable and gentle countenance, robed in iridescent blue satin with orange facings, where the atmosphere is cool and refreshing with a waterfall rushing down behind the archangel's outstretched wings.

EARTH   URIEL   WINTER
A middle aged man, grave and kind with a flowing dark beard, dressed in robes of russet, black, dark olive and citrine — the colours of Earth.

You don't need to use the Guardians unless you need a very strong circle, you can use the Elements on their own for more general workings. As the Guardians represent a more powerful way of calling the quarters you must make sure they are fully banished at the end of the working, so try to use people who are strong enough to maintain control. As with all magical workings, it is the ability to visualise and hold the visualisation that is important (together with your intent of course).

In a working circle the elements will be represented on the altar by: incense (Air), lighted candle (Fire), bowl of water (Water) and salt (Earth). There may also be quarter lights at the east, south, west, and north boundaries of the circle, this is done more often when working outside. The quarter light candles may also be in the colours of the elements: yellow, red, blue and green. In some groups or rituals, the element from the altar will be presented at each quarter during invocation, thus when invoking air the incense will be presented to all the quarters before being returned to the altar.

Below is a table listing some of the correspondences (things which represent or link) to the elements. It is not an exhaustive list, as you work with the elements you will build up your own correspondences.

EARTH ELEMENT RITUAL

This is a closed circle ritual and so should only be done with a working or training group. There should be no 'audience' and no under 18s. However, if you are working on your own there is no reason why you should not do the whole ritual for yourself. As with all Element rituals it is more effective if it can be held outdoors, in which case you can experience the Element in its natural form. However, the ritual can be adapted for indoor use, although we would advise caution if trying to do a fire Element ritual in the house.

During the ritual all the participants should go barefoot so you will need to check the ground very carefully for sharp stones and other hazards.

Altar: Green and black, rocks and crystal on it, as well as the usual Altar equipment.
Incense;   earth/wooden tones,

If you are indoors place a large bowl of earth at the base of the altar (put newspaper under bowl in case of accidents).

Introduction:

"Tonight we have gathered to come to a greater understanding of the Element of Earth, its form and substance both within us and around us" (you can have discussion of Element within group at this stage if you wish).

Summon the quarters using the Earth pentacle at each, let the invocation relate back to Earth in each case:

"I do summon and invoke thee O element of Air which passes over the Earth bringing form and change to it."

"I do summon and invoke thee O element of Fire which burns within and upon the Earth cleansing and purifying it."

"I do summon and invoke thee O element of Water, which flows within and over the Earth refreshing it and bringing forth its fruitfulness."

"I do summon and command thee O Element of Earth, the Gnomes which are your spirit. Uriel guardian of Earth be present with us and within us this night to guard over us and lend your essence to this our rite."

Request blessing of Lord and Lady, each in their winter, Crone and Lord of Death, aspects.

Seal the circle.
Use Earth related chants to raise power, for example:

The rocks, the stones
And the crystals
The power of the Earth
The power of the Earth

Each person in turn steps forward from their place in the circle and stands in front of the altar, they take a handful of earth and speak of an aspect of Earth, visualising and feeling that quality as they speak. (Go round the group until all the following aspects have been covered, further aspects may be added if group can think of them). Release earth back onto the ground (or into bowl if indoors) after speaking each phrase:

"I am solid"
"I am unyielding"
"I am patient"
"I am substance"
"I am form"
"I am the flesh of the body"
"I am the endurance of mountains"
"I am the softness of the forest floor"
"I am the baking dessert"
"I am the frozen wastes"
"I am the fertile pasture"
"I am the giver of life"
"I am the receiver of the dead"
"From me the dead are reborn"
"I am the survivor within"
"I endure forever"

Now settle them down in the circle, sitting or lying down as appropriate and use the Earth element Pathworking included in the chapter Pathworking and Guided Meditation. If you are outdoors you may wish to shorten the introductory relaxation technique to prevent them getting too cold.

The blessing and sharing of Wine and Cakes should take place next to enable the completion of the grounding process, and also as a prelude to any discussion of what has been experienced.

The elements should be banished, the Lord and Lady thanked and the circle removed. Then as with all rituals, physical tidying up, followed by going home and writing it up in your Book of Shadows.

☆ ☆ ☆ ☆ ☆

Although this is a short ritual it can be very effective if done in the right frame of mind. For this reason we would recommend that the group sets aside a series of meetings, one for each Element, at weekly intervals. You can tie them to the phases of the Moon. As a prelude there should be a meeting where all the Elements are discussed and an outline of the rituals is given. This gives everyone a chance to prepare and meditate on the aspects in advance of the workings. The four sessions should be attended by all the group, those who miss one or two elements are unlikely to gain full benefit from the growth and balance which can be achieved by completing all four.

TABLE OF ELEMENTS

ELEMENT	AIR	FIRE
Direction	East	South
Colour	Yellow	Red
Alternate Colour	Blue	Orange
Aspect	Thought	Passion
Tool	Wand	Sword
Altar	Incense	Candle
Season	Spring	Summer
	Infancy	Youth
Time	Dawn	Midday
Natural	Feathers	Candle
Sense	Smell	Sight
Guardian	Raphael	Michael
Elementals	Sylphs	Salamander
Wind	Eurus	Notus
Scents	Jasmine	Rose
	Lavender	Lotus
Crystals	Aventurine	Carnelian
	Agate	Citrine
	(not moss or tree)	Tigers Eye
Metal	Mercury	Iron/Gold
Tarot	Wands	Swords
Goddesses	Aditi	Hestia
	Nuit	Pele
Gods	Thoth	Vulcan
	Zeus	Horus

TABLE OF ELEMENTS

ELEMENT	WATER	EARTH
Direction	West	North
Colour	Blue	Green
Alternate Colour	Green	Yellow
Aspect	Emotion	Substance
Tool	Goblet	Pentacle
Altar	Chalice	Salt
Season	Autumn	Winter
	Maturity	Old Age
Time	Sunset	Midnight
Natural	Shells	Rocks
		Crystals
Sense	Taste	Touch
Guardian	Gabriel	Uriel
Elementals	Undines	Gnomes
Wind	Zephyrus	Boreas
Scents	Sandalwood	Patchouli
	Cedarwood	Musk
Crystals	Amethyst	Quartz
	Aquamarine	Jasper
	Moonstone	Jet
Metal	Silver	Lead
Tarot	Cups	Pentacles
Goddesses	Aphrodite	Gaea
	Mari	Demeter
Gods	Poseidon	Pan
	Neptune	Cernunnos

Drawing Down the Moon

Once in the month and better it be when the Moon is Full

Invocation to the Moon

Summoning a Quarter

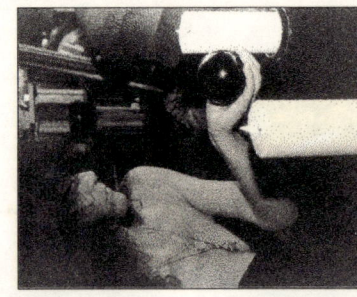

Scrying

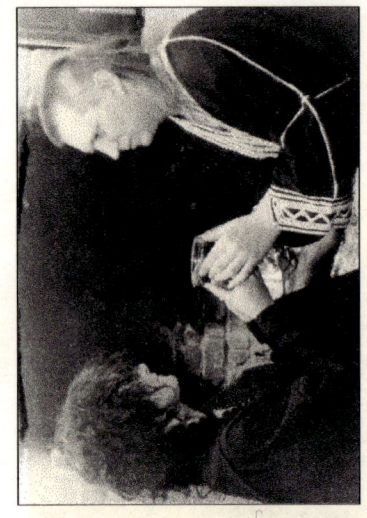

Rite of Wine & Cakes

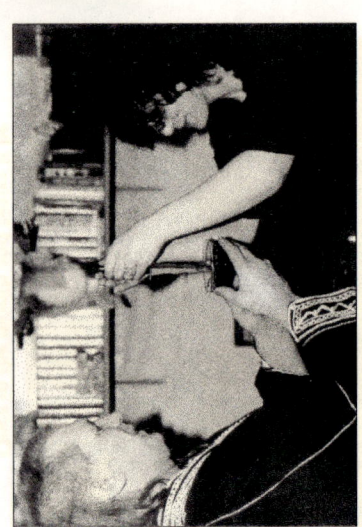

The Great Rite

The Altar

TOOLS AND EQUIPMENT

It is not necessary to have any tools or equipment at all, if you cannot put up a pentacle with your finger, you will do no better with an Athame. However, most people find that they like to acquire and use things which are special to them and to the Craft.

Anything which is used for ritual should, strictly speaking, be kept for that purpose alone, although for the Solitary with a difficult family this can be a problem. Where implements are used for ritual and then for domestic purposes they should be re-consecrated every time, many Solitaries come to their own understanding on these matters. Ritual tools should be kept secure, away from prying eyes and tampering fingers, especially anything sharp. Also, it is considered very bad manners to touch other people's tools without their express permission.

It is preferable for you to make your own tools. However, some things, like metalwork, may be better left to experts. It is also said that you should not haggle over the cost of your tools, this is not to say that you should get ripped off! If the price is unreasonable, or more than you can afford, don't pay it. In many cases the 'right' thing for you will come to you at the right time. Your tools may also be second hand, often the best things are. However, do be careful of their origins, an SS bayonet might look like a nice Athame but its history could well be dubious. Objects can be cleansed, blessed and consecrated but on the whole, if it doesn't feel right or if you have doubts, don't buy it.

So on to the list of tools and equipment. We have tried to include everything that you may come across in general reading, without getting too specialised.

ATHAME

The Witches knife, the Athame, is the extension of the finger. An Athame is a black handled, double edged knife. Strictly speaking the blade should be nine inches long and made of steel, however, variations are common. Once consecrated an Athame should not be cleaned, so when you first get it give it a good oiling before consecration as this will help to slow down the ageing process. The Athame may be decorated with sigils representative of the God and Goddess, the Craft, the owner's name or Witch name and, indeed, any other personal to the owner; again this should be done before consecration. Originally this was done to differentiate the Athame from any other knife, as all would be kept together to avoid risk of detection. Others prefer to leave theirs plain. It is used to invoke and banish, to bless and to consecrate. The only thing it should cut is the air. The Athame represents the male, on the altar and during certain rites. Many groups insist that the Athame should be blunted. This is for safety reasons, in a crowded circle accidents can happen. At home the Athame should be kept safely, even blunt it is still a knife.

You should also take great care if you intend to carry your Athame out doors, wrap it well and place it in a bag. The police are apt to consider an Athame as an offensive weapon if it is carried openly. The same precaution should be taken with the Boline and/or the sword.

BOLINE

A white handled knife with a sharp point and blade. The Boline is used for works of the Craft such as engraving sigils, preparing herbs, making wands. Unless you are likely to make a lot of use of it, the Boline is a luxury item. A Boline may be cleaned after use and will probably need sharpening from time to time. It should be kept especially secure because of its sharpness.

SWORD

This is usually owned by the Coven rather than the individual. The sword is generally plain with a crescent guard. It serves the same purposes as the Athame, but tends to be used outdoors. The sword can also be used as a symbol of Fire. In some traditions it is also used to cut the cake at a Handfasting.

PENTACLE

The five pointed star with its points touching a circle. The points symbolise the four Elements; Earth, Air, Fire and Water, together with the Spirit. The circle symbolises the magic circle cast to contain power. The pentacle symbolises man and is also a symbol of protection. It can also be used as a symbol of first degree initiation. Reversed, i.e. two points upward rather than one, the pentacle is a symbol of the Horned God and, in some groups, a symbol of second degree initiation. It is only the Americans and film makers who use a reversed pentacle as a symbol of Satanism. The pentacle is the symbol found or placed on most of the Witch's tools. A silver pentacle pendant or ring is usually the first piece of Witch jewellery that a newcomer wishes to acquire. However, don't jump to the conclusion that everyone who wears one is a Witch, it's also a piece of fashion jewellery. Conversely, it's not essential to own one to be a Witch.

OTHER JEWELLERY

Amber and Silver Ring — often given by the Coven as a symbol of second degree initiation. Amber is special as it is an organic stone, being fossilised tree resin.

Amber and Jet Necklace — worn by the High Priestess during ritual. Jet is also organic being fossilised coal.

Moonstone in Silver — worn to heighten psychic powers.

Note: Ritual jewellery is not worn for decorative purposes outside of the circle, after ritual it is put away with the other ritual equipment. Many Witches will also have a ritual ring, either amber, carnelian, jet or moonstone set in silver.

ALTAR

The Altar is where you put the things you will be using in a ritual. This can be anything from a specially made piece of furniture to a space on the window sill or mantelpiece set aside for the purpose. The Altar may be left in position permanently or set up only when required. It is usual to cover the Altar with a cloth when it is being used. The colour of this cloth will reflect the Sabbat, phase of the

Moon and/or purpose of the Ritual. On the Altar you will place the Altar candle, your representations of the Elements as well as anything else you will need during the ritual. It is important to try to get everything together before you start, to avoid having to open and close the circle to go and fetch bits and pieces you have forgotten. Try not to forget matches, a bottle opener if needed, snuffer etc. (a lot of people use a checklist to avoid the problem).

ALTAR PENTACLE

A pentagram engraved in or painted on to wood, stone or, if you're flush, brass. In addition to the symbolism mentioned above, this can be used to symbolise Earth although salt is more usual.

SALT

Salt, kept either in a small vessel or loose, is used to represent Earth on the Altar. It is the only thing which is blessed but not consecrated, as it is deemed to be pure in itself.

INCENSE

Incense, whether in sticks, cones, ropes or loose, is burnt to represent Air. Specific incenses can be chosen to honour different deities, to celebrate different Sabbats, phases of the Moon etc., or an all purpose incense can be used; Frankincense or Jasmine are good all round fragrances. Incense will require some type of stand, or holder. This does not have to be expensive, you can stand cones on a flat stone, or put sticks into a piece of wood. However, see Thurible.

THURIBLE

This is a vessel used to burn loose incense. Loose incense requires a fast igniting charcoal block in order for it to burn. This block gets extremely hot and hence requires a safe base. A Thurible is an attractive form of such a container; it is usually made of brass, occasionally wood or ceramic. Some stand on little legs, some hang from a chain. To improvise, fill a shallow dish with sand, and use this as your Thurible.

CANDLES

As with all tools of the Craft, these should be set aside for the purpose, do not use ritual candles for dinner parties or vice versa. There are two main categories of candle: firstly, your Altar candle and (if you decide to use them) quarter lights; these may be reused, ritual after ritual. Secondly, candles for specific purposes or rituals; these can only be used for that purpose. To explain; if you do a healing ritual for Anne and burn a blue candle, you cannot use that candle to do any other kind of ritual or to do a healing ritual for anyone else. Ideally it should be allowed to burn all the way down, but as you should never leave a burning candle unattended, you may need to put it out earlier. You do not blow out candles, you can either pinch them out (with moistened fingers) or use a snuffer.

Quarter lights are candles placed at the four quarters of the circle and lit during the invocation of Fire, they are mainly used in group working rather than Solitary.

WATER

A vessel with water is placed on the Altar to represent Water. If you are using water for any other purpose during the ritual it is all right to use this, unless you are using it to banish something unwanted, as this would taint the water.

CHALICE, GOBLET OR CUP

This represents the Goddess, and in most rituals will contain wine (or similar). It can be made out of brass, glass, ceramic, china or even wood. It is not used for drinking except as part of ritual. There should always be a little left of the contents to be returned to the earth, as thanks, at the end of your ritual.

ROBES

If you join a group which works robed you will need to provide yourself with one. You can make it yourself, get someone to make it for you or buy one ready made. Some Covens have specific requirements, some are more open. Check with your High Priestess or High Priest first — you don't want to labour over a robe only to find it is the wrong colour or style. However, there are some considerations you need to bear in mind anyway: it should be big enough for you to move around in freely, it should not be long enough to trip you up, it should not be so flowing that you risk setting fire to yourself, and finally, especially if you work outside, dark colours need washing less often! If you are given a free hand in choosing your robe, bear in mind most serious groups find glitter, sequins, feathers, florid embroidery etc. ostentatious, if not downright hilarious. The robe is usually girdled by a cord of the same or a contrasting colour; remember this needs to be long enough to go round your middle and tie up, it should not restrict your breathing.

CORDS
There are many types of cords; one four foot six inches in length is traditionally used to draw the circle. One will be used in initiation to bind the initiate and this or another may be used to take the measure. Coloured cords are used in cord magic, which involves tying a series of knots to cast a spell.

BOOK OF SHADOWS
There is no such thing as THE Book of Shadows. There seems little doubt these days that the Gardnerian Book of Shadows was written by Gardner himself. Our predecessors would not have kept a Book of Shadows; most couldn't read or write, most couldn't afford the paper and few would have been stupid enough to keep a document which, if discovered, was guaranteed to result in the death penalty. Each Witch keeps his or her own. It is a journal of your rituals, workings, experiences and feelings. You will keep recipes for herbal and magical remedies and the results you get from them, so that you can use them again when they work. You may like to keep tables of correspondences, moon phases, etc. in it too. There are some rituals which you may copy down from other sources, such as the Book of Shadows of your Coven or High Priestess or from

published sources. The purpose of keeping a Book of Shadows is to have a record of what works for you, of how you felt after doing a particular ritual and also, in a training Coven, so that your High Priestess or High Priest can make sure you do not get yourself into trouble. They don't mark it like homework, but they do use it to guide and advise. Traditionally your Book of Shadows should be handwritten, but many Witches nowadays keep some, if not all, of it on computer. Whichever you do, remember this should never be allowed to get into the hands of anyone other than yourself, your trainer, and in due course, those you train.

WAND

Wands are generally hand made from fallen wood. You do not hack bits off living trees to make them. The wood may be chosen for its own significance or just because it's a suitable shape and size. A wand may be decorated and adorned in any way you wish (using natural materials, no plastic please). Wands are generally a symbol of air, but wands can also be made for the other elements or for other purposes such as healing. A wand will be used for invocation and banishing or to direct power.

STAFF

A staff is used to control and direct energies in a similar way to a wand. However, it is much larger. Made in much the same way as a wand, it is useful if one end is pointed as it is frequently used by placing it in the ground.

CAULDRON

Traditionally, the cauldron was used to brew things in. Nowadays it is used to contain fire, either indoors or out. Again this is something usually owned by the Coven rather than the individual.

BROOMSTICK

A symbol of fertility. The pole representing the phallus, and often it's the brush end carved to resemble one, the brush representing the female. The broomstick is sometimes used to sweep clear the circle prior to ritual. The broomstick is also jumped at Handfasting to bring about a fertile relationship. It used to be used to indicate whether other Witches were welcome to call. Brush down means it's not a good time.

SCOURGE
The scourge represents the sorrows of this world and is used in (mainly Gardnerian) initiations. It should not cause injury to the initiate, but should be felt. Often the thongs are made from cord or leather and the handle of wood.

PESTLE AND MORTAR
The mortar is a bowl, usually small and rounded, the pestle is the instrument you use to pound or grind the ingredients within the mortar. If you are seriously into herb lore and healing you will want to grind your own herbs. For this you will need some form of pestle and mortar. Again, you can purchase an elaborate one, hunt down an antique one or simply use a wooden spoon and mixing bowl. Whatever you decide, make sure that you keep it scrupulously clean. Many of your preparations will be intended for application or eating; you don't want to poison anyone. Also traces of previous preparations may interfere with the magical intent of the current one.

TOOLS OF DIVINATION
All Witches practice some form of divination or scrying. That is they look into the future or seek to look into the unknown. Whilst this comes naturally to some, most people find that they need the assistance of some form of tool. Generally this will act as a focus point for the concentration, letting the subconscious come to the fore. We all of us have this talent, but in most cases it is suppressed early in life. There can be very few people who cannot remember a small child stating an embarrassing truth which they had no means of knowing, only to be immediately hushed by a parent! So learning to scry is once more a question or re-discovering a latent talent, and trusting what we feel. Twenty years ago, tools of divination were

not readily available, nowadays sets of Tarot cards and even ouija boards are available from bookstores, mail order and other outlets. There are many excellent books on Divination available and we do not intend to give here more than a brief outline of some of the more well known forms of scrying:

TAROT – the Tarot is a deck of cards. Originally produced for profit by monks for gamblers it was, understandably, banned by the church. The deck is comprised of four suits: wands (or staves), cups, swords and pentacles (or coins). These are called the Minor Arcana and are very like the suits in an ordinary deck of playing cards, except that there are fourteen in each suit, the extra one being the Knight. In addition there is the Major Arcana, or picture cards; there are twenty-two of these, making seventy-eight cards in all. The Major Arcana represents our passage through life. The Tarot is one of the more recent forms of Divination as its history cannot be reliably traced back much further than the 13th Century. Currently there are over 200 different Tarot packs available on the market, some of which have slightly more or less cards than the traditional form outlined above. There are also many decks of self development and self exploration cards which, whilst superficially similar to the Tarot, may have only a fraction of the number of cards. These newer versions are no less valid, but they are not Tarot.

CRYSTAL BALL – popularly associated with the Gypsy fortune-teller, the crystal ball is a very attractive tool. However, a lot of people find it very difficult to use. Made of lead crystal, rock crystal or polished gemstone, crystal balls can be extremely expensive. A more traditional Witch's tool is the Dark Mirror.

DARK MIRROR – take a bowl of water and add some black ink. Arrange it so that no reflection falls on the surface (a darkened room helps), compose yourself and look deep into the water.

In time, and with practice, you may see images forming in the depths. Some Witches like to perform this with the light of the Full Moon reflected on the surface. Alternatively, take a concave piece of glass and hold it over a smoking candle so that the outside is covered in black, arrange this on a stand and gaze into the inner surface. But be warned, the latter method can be very messy. If you find you can use a Dark Mirror, then you might want to consider finding the money for a Crystal Ball.

RUNES – the Whisperers. This is an Ancient Norse / Germanic form of communication. Unlike our alphabet, each symbol in the runic alphabet carries a wealth of meaning: sound, smell, taste, emotion, plant or animal. In a traditional set of Runes there are twenty-four marked pieces (made of stone, wood, ceramic or other natural product) and one unmarked piece, representing Wyrd or fate. Again, there are many different versions available on the market, although we would caution the purchaser against any set with overtly Christian meanings. These can be worse than useless as whatever your cast, the reading invariably ends up telling you to work harder, be more considerate and wishes you love and light! Hardly the intention of our pre-Christian ancestors.

OGHAM – the Celtic Tree Alphabet. This predates the Runes and was originally a tool of communication. Each character is a series of cuts made vertically in a piece of wood, messages are intended to be read from bottom to top — the same way a tree grows. It also carries a wealth of meaning in each of its characters.

TEA LEAVES – a much underrated method of Divination, the tea leaves are an excellent starting ground for anyone wishing to learn. They are cheap, convenient and you can generally practice on your friends without arousing suspicion or concern. The method is simple; make tea in a pot (with leaves, not bags!), pour into a cup (milk and sugar to taste), drink down to about 1cm from the bottom (do not swallow the leaves — it makes them harder to read!). Swirl the cup a couple of times to get the leaves back into suspension and invert the cup over the saucer. Examine the leaves left in the base of the cup and use your intuition to interpret the pictures they form.

PENDULUM — a weight of silver, crystal, wood or stone is suspended on a chain or string, in such a way that it moves freely. This is 'programmed' by the user to determine the direction of swing for the three responses: yes, no, maybe. Simple, direct questions can then be answered.

CLAIRVOYANCE — if the Ogham, Tarot or tea leaves are regarded as tools of divination, then clairvoyance is Divination without any tools. Clairvoyance literally means clear sight, however, the clear vision involved is on an inner, not an outer level. Clairvoyance should not be confused with mediumship. Clairvoyants do not talk to spirits from the 'other side', mediums do. Witches do not believe in calling on the spirits of the dead, and so do not generally practise mediumship, although they will act as go between should a spirit present itself during a reading. Psychic, by the way, is an umbrella term for anyone who practises any of the forms of Divination. Most Witches have the ability for far seeing; where this comes from is debatable, some believe it is genetically inherited. In gypsy families it is accepted that the gift of the 'sight' is handed down from mother to child. In more traditional groups of Witches the term Witch blood is often used and the belief that the gift can skip several generations before becoming apparent again is held as the norm.

CIRCLE WORK

The circle is cast to keep in the power raised, and to keep out unwanted forces. Traditionally the circle is nine feet across, and many groups will keep a cord four foot six inches in length for use in casting the circle. One end would be held in place in the centre of the circle, the other end would be walked around to describe the circle, either by use of chalk or by scratching in the earth. However, if you are working indoors it is often impractical to have a nine foot circle, in which case your circle should be large enough for the people concerned to operate in. A circle should be cast for all magical workings, it is not usually cast at the Sabbats. Sabbats are celebrations, not times of magical working.

Before commencing to work in a circle you should comply with *The Five Necessities:*

> **INTENTION** – your intentions must be true, you must be able to focus on what you are about to do, don't start out with half an idea or an unformed wish. Many people have discovered the need to be careful what they wish for, when they get something that's what they asked for, but is not what they wanted.
>
> **PREPARATION** – you must be properly prepared, mentally and physically, get everything you will need together before you start.
>
> **INVOCATION** – the mighty ones must be invoked, the Quarters must be summoned, the Lord and Lady invited.
>
> **CONSECRATION** – the circle must be properly cast, there are no short cuts.
>
> **PURIFICATION** – you must be purified, this refers more to your state of mind than your body. Whilst it is nice to be physically clean for ritual, it's not essential. However, your mind should

be pure, free from mental and emotional distractions. Having said that, many people find that a warm bath is the ideal place in which to soak away all the mundane cares and to prepare mentally for the work ahead. Do not drink alcohol or take drugs before a ritual. If you are unwell or over-tired, do not attempt to work magic. You must be able to focus and concentrate.

The following must be covered for any working:

Prepare yourself
Prepare the altar
Bless the salt, consecrate the other elements
Summon the Quarters
Invite the Lord and Lady
Seal the circle
Perform the ritual
Banish the Quarters
Thank the Lord and Lady
Remove the circle
Earth yourself
Tidy up
Write it up

When working in a Coven you will find that you share most of the above steps with the other members. However, when one person invokes an element, they are doing it on behalf of the group, and everyone present must visualise the element and pentacle during the invocation, and the circle when it is drawn. You are not watching a play put on for your entertainment, you must participate, otherwise you will get nothing out of it. Some groups require everyone to draw the invoking and banishing pentacles. In which case, the rest of the group stand behind the person nominated and perform the same actions at the same time.

PREPARE YOURSELF

You are responsible for preparing yourself. Leave your emotional baggage at home, do not come with secondary purposes in mind, such as the intention to get the money back you loaned another group member or the desire to start up a 'meaningful relationship' with someone in the circle. Not only will you spoil it for yourself, you will also affect the atmosphere for everyone else. If you cannot free your head of distractions, have a word with the High Priest or High Priestess, they may be able to organise a banishing or meditation to assist you. Be honest with yourself about this and try not to leave it until 30 seconds before the ritual starts. There are two short rituals which can be performed after the circle is cast which can help the group or individual prepare: Banishing of Unwanted Influences and Self Blessing. Both of these can be performed on their own or as the start to further work, they are included in the chapter 'Rites and Rituals'.

When you arrive for ritual be aware that others will have put a lot of effort into getting everything ready, writing the ritual, preparing handouts, moving furniture, laying the altar, preparing for feasting afterwards and also undertaking their own personal preparation. Arrive on time and peacefully. Pay a last visit to the bathroom if needed. Undress or change into your robe, settle down quietly and (where applicable) review your part or role, this is a good time to spend a few minutes meditating on the purpose of the ritual. Allow others to settle too. This is not a good time to start discussions, debates or to ask questions; save them for afterwards. If you have questions pertaining to the ritual you are about to take part in, you should have asked them earlier! However, select the person who looks least harassed to ask them of. It's worth mentioning that, had you taken notes when the ritual was explained to you, you would know what you're going to do and why. There will be times when a ritual is not explained in advance; there are reasons for this, so keep your curiosity in check and all should be revealed.

LAYING THE ALTAR

The altar will be either in the centre of the circle or at the North point. On it will be

Altar Candle(s), Pentacle, Salt, Incense and holder, Water, and a separate candle for Fire if one is used. Matches! Your Athame (if you have one) and equipment for the ritual. Often it is easier to make a list before you start and check it off as you go, don't forget to be practical, you need a corkscrew for wine etc. The Altar Candle(s) and incense should be lit prior to starting. Remember Altar Candle(s) (and where used, quarter lights) may be used over and over, (but keep them for ritual, don't use them for parties as well). Ritual candles may not.

HANDLING AN ATHAME

An Athame is a knife, whether blunted or not. Use it carefully, Coven members do not take kindly to being stabbed or cut because you turned round fast, or let it fly out of your hand!

The correct way to hold the Athame is in your strong hand; most people are right handed. Place your forefinger down the flat face of the blade, not the sharp edge, and grip firmly with the rest of your hand. If you are in any doubt ask your High Priestess or High Priest to show you.

Once consecrated, your Athame should never be cleaned. You may apply oil to it to help protect it if you wish, but cleaning will remove the build up of energy. You may wish to obtain or make a sheaf for it; this is useful as it protects the blade and the Athame can then be hung from your belt when not being used. Remember to bring your Athame to all rituals.

An Athame is a personal thing, so never handle another person's without asking first.

BLESSING AND CONSECRATION OF THE ELEMENTS

The salt is blessed as it is already pure and does not need consecration. Draw an invoking pentacle over it with your finger or Athame saying something along the lines of "I bless thee O element of Earth to make thee fit for use in this our rite", then kiss your finger, the one pointing down the Athame, and say "Blessed Be". At this point the rest of the group should echo your "Blessed Be", and everyone should mean it. You can use different or more detailed words if you wish, but the important thing is that your will should be focused and your intention clear. The other Elements are consecrated and blessed; "I consecrate thee and bless thee O Element of Air (Fire, Water) to drive out all impurities and make thee fit for this our rite". Again the invoking pentacle is drawn over or into the Element, the finger kissed and "Blessed Be". As with any part of any ritual or working, take your time, do not hurry. Slowly, carefully performed rites are far better than hurried sloppy ones.

INVOKING THE QUARTERS
The quarters are invoked in the following order: Air, Fire, Water and Earth. Each quarter is summoned using the invoking pentacle of that Element. Standing at the appropriate point of the circle; Air – East, Fire – South, Water – West, Earth – North, you centre yourself and visualise the Element (Elemental or Guardian if you' re using Elementals or Guardians). Draw and visualise the invoking pentacle with your Athame. Remember the pentacle has five points but takes six strokes to draw as you have to seal it, and is finished off with a point in the centre. Again there are no set words but you should say something along the lines of "I summon and invoke thee O Element of Air, to watch over us, guard and protect us during these our rites". Kiss your finger and say "Blessed Be". Use a loud firm voice, you are summoning the elements, not sharing a secret with them. The rest of the group should visualise with you, and in some circles should draw the pentacle too, they all echo your "Blessed Be". In some groups the Element is then taken from the Altar, presented to all the quarters (its own first) and then returned to the Altar.

Again, take your time, do it with feeling and make it effective. With practice you and the group should be able to 'see' the Elements and the pentacles in place. You may find that some groups prefer to raise the circle first, in which case, when working with them, that is what you do.

CALLING UPON THE LORD AND LADY

You invite the Lord and Lady. You do not summon or command them. Facing the altar and North, centre yourself, raise both arms, visualise the Goddess and the God and say "I ask the presence of the Lord and the Lady (or whatever names you wish to use) to watch over us, to guide and protect us during these our rites. Blessed Be". The group again echoes your Blessed Be. You can use your own words but the intention should remain the same.

SEALING THE CIRCLE

With your Athame, start at North and draw a line around the outer edge of the circle, going deosil. You should envisage an electric-blue light coming from the tip of your Athame and remaining around the circumference of the circle, this light should then be visualised as forming a sphere containing the circle. Whilst you do this you speak "I conjure this circle to be a place of power and protection, a place between the worlds and a time outside of time". Again, use your own words, ensure that the circle is complete by overlapping the start and finish at the East point.

If at any time it becomes necessary to leave the circle, you will need to cut a doorway with your Athame, exit, seal the doorway with your Athame, and reverse the process to get back in. However, if you prepared properly, this should rarely be necessary.

PERFORMING THE RITUAL

You do not work ritual for fun, it is serious. Take it seriously. Yes, there will be the occasional moments of humour, when someone makes a mistake or says the wrong thing, but it is not a party or social event.

You do not work ritual for practice! Every time in the circle is the real thing, there are no 'dress rehearsals'. In the authors' Coven, individuals are encouraged to put the circle up and perform a Self Blessing as practice. Ensure that you stay focused on the purpose of the ritual. This is hard work, you should feel tired at the end of a ritual, if you don't then you're probably not putting enough in to it.

At all times move deosil (clockwise) in the circle, unless specifically instructed to do otherwise.

Take it slowly, do not rush it. Hurry makes for mistakes.

When working in the circle, try to avoid bits of paper. There are no set words. You use the words to express your intent, so as long as they do that, it's fine. It's far better for you to use your concentration on your intention than on precise wording. If you fluff it, stop, centre yourself, and start again.

If, for any reason, you find yourself unable to continue, when working with a group, do not disrupt the others. Centre yourself and concentrate on what they are doing. If working on your own, banish what you have invoked, thank the Lord and Lady if you have invited them and generally clear up after yourself.

BANISHING THE QUARTERS

Stand at the appropriate quarter, centre yourself. With your Athame describe the banishing pentacle, visualising the pentacle and the Element (Elemental or Guardian) going. Say something like "I banish thee O Element of Air, with thanks for being present and watching over us during these our rites. Hail and Farewell." Kiss your finger "Blessed Be". The rest of the group should also visualise with you and echo your "Blessed Be". The Elements are banished in the same order, and by the same people, as they were summoned.

THANK THE LORD AND LADY

Stand facing the altar and north, and centre yourself. Raise both arms and say something like " I give thanks to the Lord and Lady for guiding, protecting and watching over us during these our rites." Kiss your finger. "Blessed Be." Again, visualise them going, and the group echoes your "Blessed Be".

REMOVE THE CIRCLE

With your Athame, draw around the circle, visualising the circle vanishing. Say something like "I remove the circle of protection. Our circle is broken but not ended." Kiss your finger "Blessed Be", echoed by the group.

EARTH YOURSELF

Have something to eat or drink. This is essential. You must return your awareness to the here and now. This is why there should always be something provided after every working, even if it's only tea and biscuits. Most Covens will ensure that the responsibility for provisions, and the cost, is shared amongst members. You do not have to spend much time or money, but do make sure you take your turn.

TIDY UP

Clear away – do not leave your bits and pieces in someone else's home without permission. You should feel strongly enough about your ritual equipment to take care of it. Left over altar wine and cakes should be returned to the earth as thanks, using household plumbing is fine.

WRITE IT UP

As soon as you can, write up the ritual in your Book of Shadows. Don't be tempted to think that you will remember it and can do it later. Very few people can do this successfully. Most of us just make a rod for our own backs by leaving it until we have more time, feel more like it etc. You should enter the outline of the ritual, your part(s) in the ritual, your experiences and feelings. Do it clearly so that you and anyone who checks it can read it. Avoid use of codes and shorthand. Never include the name of other group members or location of the ritual. Do include the date of the ritual, it's purpose and the phase of the Moon. Your Book of Shadows should be made available to the High Priest or High Priestess whenever they ask to see it.

WORKING ON YOUR OWN

It is tempting, especially when starting out, to work ritual for all sorts of reasons. Remember magic is not a substitute for living: If you want someone to talk to you, try introducing yourself instead of working a ritual. If you want to pass a test or examination, study!

Your first step is to decide what you intend to do, and formulate it carefully. If you are in a Coven check it through with your High Priestess or High Priest, before you do the working. Remember they are there to guide and assist you. They may advise that it should be done in the group or on your own, there will be good reasons for this. One of the quickest ways to attract the wrath of your High Priestess and/or High Priest is to play with magic. Odd though it seems to most newcomers to the Craft, the decision to become a Witch does not make you infallible! Clearing up the mess after unwisely, or ill prepared, rituals is one of the banes of running a training group. In addition, the inexperienced Witch is as likely as not to achieve the opposite of what they set out to do. If you must practice, use the Self Blessing as the centre of your ritual.

Next you need to decide when. You will need to refer to the phases of the Moon, although the Full Moon can be used for almost any magical working. The days of the week, and indeed, hours of the day are linked with the planets, so that you can enhance the influences around your working by selecting day and time. For this you need to refer to the table of planetary hours. You also need to plan around the other members of your household.

At your chosen time you need to ensure that you will have privacy and no interruptions, either in person or by phone! If you have pets it may be safer to shut them out of the room to avoid distraction and worries about candles. However, they are also creatures of the Goddess and the God and are thus allowed to enter and exit a circle freely. People under 18 should not be within a cast circle except under very special circumstances.

The Pentacle

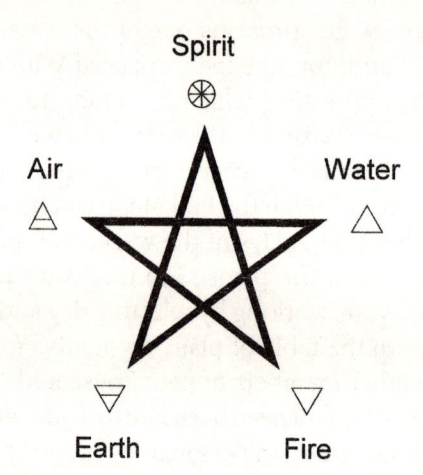

Spirit

Air

Water

Earth

Fire

Elemental Pentacles

INVOKING		BANISHING
	EARTH	
	AIR	
	FIRE	
	WATER	

RAISING POWER

One of the first things done in a working circle is the raising of power. The methods of raising power are traditionally known as the Eight Fold Path, and the symbol for this is found on many ritual implements. It is an eight-spoked wheel without a rim. Power raising is important in any ritual, when done in a group of people it has the effect of producing more power than the sum of the individuals, a bit like adding six two volt batteries together and obtaining twenty volts instead of twelve. The role of the High Priestess or High Priest is to control and focus that power so that it reaches it's intended destination.

THE EIGHT FOLD PATH:

>**MEDITATION OR CONCENTRATION** – this can be done using pathworking or guided visualisation. The group or individual may use a focus point, such as a tarot card or a candle flame. Or they may use a structured countdown system, like the Chakra colour system.
>
>**CHANTS, SPELLS, INVOCATIONS** – chanting repetitively is an excellent system with a group as it brings the group mind in tune rapidly. It doesn't matter what the chant is "Zap washes whiter" would do the trick so long as the intent is true. However, there are many Wiccan and Pagan chants available, or you can write your own.
>
>**ASTRAL PROJECTION OR TRANCE** – this takes time to master and can be dangerous for the inexperienced, as when you are out of your body it can be open to other forces.
>
>**INCENSE, WINE, AIDS TO RELEASE THE SPIRIT** – there's a fine line between an aid to release the spirit and getting legless! The circle is no place for the drunk or stoned.

DANCING – especially circle dancing, is very effective and can be combined with chanting.

BLOOD CONTROL, USE OF THE CORDS – this can be risky with the inexperienced as it's all too easy to overdo it and end up a news headline. A safer version is to use bio-feedback techniques, this involves controlling blood supply by the use of the mind.

THE SCOURGE – the causing of a certain amount of pain will heighten consciousness and awareness. Gardnerian Witches make a lot of use of the scourge, either actually or in token.

THE GREAT RITE – the Great Rite is performed symbolically between the Priest and Priestess to raise power for the group. The wine thus consecrated is shared by the whole group. The Great Rite actual, is the act of sexual penetration between the male and the female. It is performed at the third degree initiation. It does not involve full sexual intercourse, unless the couple concerned are already part of a loving relationship.

Raising power must be done in a closed circle, otherwise there is nothing to prevent the power dissipating even as it is built. The energy thus produced comes from all of the group and it is noticeable that, when successful, everyone will be exhausted and elated. If you do not feel this way after power raising, you have not been working hard enough.

In group working the most commonly used method of raising power is through the combination of chant and dance. Everyone will dance deosil around the circle, holding hands makes for greater control and stability, whilst chanting one or two simple chants. The faster the circle spins the quicker the energy will be raised. There are many versions of the circle dance and once a group has mastered the basic technique they will often develop their own style.

POWER RAISING THROUGH CHAKRA COLOUR COUNTDOWN

The seven Chakras are the major energy centres of the body. Study of the Chakras is worthwhile, but for the purpose of power raising you do not need to know a great deal, simply concentrate on the part of the body and the colour. Focus and intent are all.

CHAKRA	PLACE ON BODY	COLOUR
Muladhara	Base of Spine	Red
Swadhisthana	Navel	Orange
Manipura	Solar Plexus	Yellow
Anahata	Heart	Green
Vishudda	Throat	Blue
Ajna	Brow/Third Eye	Violet
Sahasrara	Crown	Orchid or White

Method:

Centre yourself, think of a red disc spinning deosil (clockwise) at the base of your spine. When you have this visualised go on to start the next disc spinning, orange at your navel, get both discs spinning before you move on to the yellow at your solar plexus and so on. You may find it's a bit like a fairground plate-spinner — you sometimes have to go back to keep the discs spinning.

When you have red, orange, yellow, green, blue and violet going (yes, all at the same time) visualise the power pouring out of the top of your head (your crown) as an orchid-white light, it fountains out over your body and goes back to feed the red disc. When you are ready and everything feels stable, you direct the energy out from your crown towards your intention.

To close down afterwards, envisage white pouring down from your crown and covering each disc in turn. As each disc is covered, it stops spinning. Continue all the way down, stopping before you cover red; you do not close down your base Chakra. You are then finished.

Don't worry if you don't get it right first time, it takes practise to master the technique. If you wish to practise, do so, but remember if you only get as far as, say, green, you must close down the Chakras you have opened when you stop. Leaving Chakras open leaves your psyche open to external influences. However, as it involves visualisation and no other props, it is one of the most useful techniques to learn. When experienced, you can do this in a minute or less.

RITES AND RITUALS

A Ritual is a series of thoughts, words and actions performed to bring about a specific result. A series of Rites go to make up the Ritual.

In Gardnerian Witchcraft, rituals are laid down and followed precisely; the same ritual will be performed for say, Lammas, each and every year. In the Alexandrian tradition there is more emphasis on writing rituals afresh, so that, although the intent is the same, the words and actions would vary from year to year, and from group to group. Instinctual (or Traditional) Witches may follow either system, as may Solitaries.

In some Covens only initiates may take an active part, non-initiates simply look and learn. In some groups only those who have taken their second degree (or third) may participate. Other groups prefer to spread the active roles so that everyone has a chance to learn and experience. The authors share the latter viewpoint, we feel that, unless a particularly difficult or private ritual is undertaken, that as many of the group as possible should take part. Obviously this can give rise to occasions when mistakes are made, and not a few moments of laughter. However, we believe that our Gods and Goddesses have a sense of humour.

The main categories of ritual are:

>SABBATS – eight throughout the year, these are celebratory, the circle is open and there is no magical working.

>ESBATS – the Full Moons, thirteen throughout the year. These are primarily an act of worship and celebration, sometimes they will include magical workings such as healing and scrying. The circle is Closed.

>MAGICAL – timed to the appropriate Moon phase and with reference to the planetary day and hour. These rituals are designed to bring about a specific purpose, this includes ritual

pathworkings, healing, and the acquisition and enhancement of qualities. Again the circle is Closed.

In any ritual where the circle is closed there will be an element of power raising. The power raised comes, as we have said before, from the individuals within the circle. This is the reason you should not work ritual when you are unwell, whether physically or mentally, pregnant, taking drugs or medication, or under any other circumstances when you are not fully at one with yourself and in control of your thoughts and emotions. You must be strictly honest with yourself and with your High Priestess or High Priest. Some groups will allow people in this position to attend the working group, but to sit out, in order that they do not miss out on the learning aspect of working. Other groups apply the rules more strictly and do not allow attendance in any form. However hard this may seem, the direction of the High Priestess or High Priest must be accepted. It's no use faking it, either, they will know.

There are abundant published sources from which rituals may be taken, so in this book we will give only a few: the Banishment of Unwanted Influences, Self Blessing, the Rite of Wine and Cakes and Drawing Down the Moon.

BANISHMENT OF UNWANTED INFLUENCES
In addition to the usual altar set-up you will need a large bowl of water. After the circle has been cast the water in this bowl is consecrated and blessed in the same way as the water on the altar was done at the start.

This bowl is then taken round the circle, deosil, stopping at each person. As the bowl of water reaches each one, it is held in front of them and they immerse all their fingers in the water. As they do so they speak "I banish all unwanted feelings and influences into this water, that my mind, body and spirit may be pure", or similar words, if desired they may actually speak of the things which are disrupting them. They visualise all such thoughts, feelings and emotions draining through their arms and hands and into the water. When they are ready they remove their fingers from the water and say "Blessed Be", which is echoed by the group.

The bowl is then taken to the next person and the process repeated. Some groups like to have the bowl carrier followed by a towel carrier, so that hands may be dried. When the bowl has been all the way round the circle someone should take the bowl from the bowl carrier so that they also take their turn. The bowl is then placed out of the way.

On no account should this water be used for any other purpose afterwards, it contains all the unwanted and undesirable thoughts, feelings and emotions of the group. As with all ritual, if undertaken seriously and with intent, this is very effective.

SELF BLESSING

This ritual is performed to bring the blessing of the Goddess on the individual.

In addition to the usual altar set up you will need a goblet of wine and a goblet of water. Consecrate and bless the wine and the water as you did the elements at the start. Pour some of the wine into the water. If you wish you may use an anointing oil, in which case this should be consecrated and blessed.

> Kneeling in front of the altar, with your chosen anointing medium, take some deep breaths to centre yourself then visualise the Goddess, then:
>
> Dip fingers in the water, anoint your eyes and say :
> "Blessed be my eyes, that I may see thy path"
>
> Dip fingers in the water, anoint your nose and say :
> "Blessed be my nose, that I may breathe thy essence"
>
> Dip fingers in the water, anoint your mouth and say :
> "Blessed be my mouth, that I may speak of thee"

> Dip fingers in the water, anoint your heart/breast and say :
> "Blessed be my breast, that I may be faithful in thy works"
>
> Dip fingers in the water, anoint your loins if male or womb if female and say :
> "Blessed be my loins/womb, which bring forth the life of man, as thou hast brought forth life eternal"
>
> Dip fingers in the water, anoint your feet and say :
> "Blessed be my feet, that I may walk in thy ways"
>
> Again visualise the Goddess and say: "Bless me Mother, for I am thy child"
> "Blessed Be". The group will, of course, echo your "Blessed Be".

Remain and meditate, when you are ready, stand, move deosil around the circle to return to your place so that another may take their place in front of the Altar.

THE RITE OF WINE AND CAKES

The Rite of Wine and Cakes is performed towards the end of a ritual and involves the blessing of wine and special biscuits which are then shared around the group. It is usually performed at the Esbats and minor Sabbats. At the major Sabbats the Great Rite is performed. On the altar you will need a goblet of wine (usually red) and a plate with enough biscuits for everyone to have one each. The biscuits are traditionally crescent shaped to represent the Moon. Occasionally you may get someone whose dietary restrictions do not allow them to eat biscuits, a slice of fruit may be substituted for these people. Again there are many versions of this Rite and it is the intent, not the wording, which is important. The Rite can also be performed by one person on their own.

The Priest and Priestess, it does not have to be the High Priestess and the High Priest, should stand in front of the altar, facing the rest of the group, with the Priestess on the Priest's left.

The Wine

> The Priest holds the goblet of wine up to the group and says: "Behold the cup, the Cauldron of Cerridwen, the fount of knowledge, and symbol of the Goddess". Still holding the goblet he turns towards the Priestess.
>
> The Priestess takes the Athame and shows it to the group saying:
> "Behold the Athame." Still holding the Athame she turns towards the Priest, so that they are facing each other in front of the altar and the group.
>
> Using the Athame, the Priestess describes the invoking pentacle over the wine, finishing by dipping the point of the Athame into the wine and holding it there. She says "By this Athame, symbol of the Horned God I consecrate and bless this wine, that all may share in the wisdom of the Goddess."
>
> The Athame is then replaced on the Altar.
>
> The Priest then hands the goblet to the Priestess with the words "With Perfect Love and Perfect Trust" and kisses her once on each cheek, she replies "With Perfect Love and Perfect Trust" kisses him on each cheek and takes a sip of the wine. The Priestess then turns to the next person in the circle (deosil) and passes on the goblet saying "With Perfect Love and Perfect Trust" and kissing them on each cheek, they respond as she did to the Priest. In this way the goblet is passed around the whole group, deosil, until it returns to the Priest who drinks and then replaces the goblet on the altar.

The Cakes

The Priest takes the plate of cakes and says :

"We bless these cakes as a token of our sacrifice and ask the Old Gods to be with us until we meet again. Thus with wine and cakes we pledge ourselves to them and to each other."

The Priestess takes the Athame and traces an invoking pentacle over the cakes.

The cakes are passed around in the same way as the goblet, with an exchange of kisses and of the words "With Perfect Love and Perfect Trust".

In a small group, say less than six, it is often better to let the wine return to the altar before commencing with the cakes.

DRAWING DOWN THE MOON

Drawing Down the Moon is the ritual performed by the Coven at the Full Moon. Some groups will perform it at every Full Moon, others will do so only from time to time. In some groups only the High Priest and High Priestess will take part, in others the roles are shared amongst the members in order that all have the opportunity to experience it and in order that the members will bond together more fully.

In Drawing Down the Moon the Priest calls down the essence of the Goddess into the Priestess. The Priestess, thus inspired, will then deliver the Charge of the Goddess. The Charge is a poetic statement of direction for the Coven. Some groups insist that it is learned and delivered verbatim, others prefer to encourage spontaneity, to actually let the Goddess speak through the Priestess. There are many versions of Drawing Down the Moon, and indeed of the Charge of the Goddess. Here we give a well known version of Drawing Down the Moon, a Solitary method, and three versions of the Charge.

The Priestess stands facing the Moon, the Priest stands in front of her with his back to the group. Both are standing in the North of the Circle. The Priestess stands with her arms outspread.

The Priest gives the Priestess *The Five-fold Blessing:*

"Blessed be thy feet which have brought thee in these ways"
he kneels then he kisses her right foot then her left

"Blessed Be thy knees that shall kneel at the sacred altar"
he kisses her right, then left knee

"Blessed be thy womb without which we should not be"
he kisses her just above the pubic hair

"Blessed Be they breasts, formed in beauty"
he stands then he kisses her right, then left breast

"Blessed Be thy lips that shall utter the sacred words"
he kisses her on the lips and they embrace full length

The Priest then performs *Drawing Down the Moon,* during which the Priestess concentrates on evoking (bringing into herself) the spirit of the Goddess:

With his right forefinger the Priest then touches the Priestess on the right breast, left breast, womb and right breast whilst saying:
"I invoke thee and call upon thee, mighty Mother of us all, bringer of all fruitfulness, by seed and root, by stem and bud, by leaf and flower and fruit, do I invoke thee to descend upon this, the body of thy servant and Priestess."

The Priest kneels again and spreads his arms outwards and downwards and says:

"Hail Aradia! from the Amalthean horn. Pour forth thy store of love. I lowly bend before thee, I adore thee to the end. With loving sacrifice thy shrine adorn. Thy foot is to my lip" he kisses her feet. "My prayer upborn upon the rising incense smoke. Then spend thine ancient love O Mighty One, descend to aid me who without thee am forlorn."

The Priest rises and faces the group
"Listen to the words of the Great Mother; she, who of old, was also called among men Artemis, Astarte, Athene, Dione, Melusine, Aphrodite, Cerridwen, Dana, Arianrhod, Isis, Bride and by many other names."

The Priestess then faces the group and delivers *The Charge of the Goddess:*

"Whenever ye have need of any thing, once in the month and better it be when the moon is full, then shall ye assemble in some secret place and worship the spirit of me, who art Queen of all Witches. There shall ye assemble, ye who are fain to learn all sorcery, and yet have not won its deepest secrets; to these shall I teach things that are as yet unknown. And ye shall be free from slavery, and as a sign that ye be really free ye shall be naked in your Rites; and ye shall dance, sing, feast, make music and love all in my praise. For mine is the ecstasy of the spirit, and mine is also joy on earth, for my law is love unto all things. Keep pure your highest ideal, strive ever towards it; let naught stop you or turn you aside. For mine is the secret door which opens on to the land of youth, and mine is the cup of the wine of life, and the Cauldron of Cerridwen, which is the Holy Grail of immortality. I am the gracious Goddess, who gives the gift of joy of life unto the heart of man. Upon earth I give knowledge of the spirit eternal, and beyond death, I give peace and freedom and reunion with those who have gone before. Nor do I demand sacrifice, for behold I am the gracious Mother of all living, and my love is poured out upon the earth. And thou who thinkest to seek for me, know thy seeking and yearning shall avail thee not, for unless thou knowest the mystery; that if that which thou seekest, thou findest not within thee, then thou shalt never find it without thee. For behold, I have been with thee from the beginning; and I am that which is attained at the end of desire."

When this ritual is performed properly the whole group will share in the blessing of the Goddess and all will feel benefit from it. The effect is lessened considerably by the use of bits of paper, it is better that the intention and content is right rather than reading a script. However, for the Priestess delivering the Charge for the first time, she may feel more comfortable if the words are available in case she loses her place. In this instance another person should be there to hold the 'script' in suitably large print at a sensible height.

The Thunder, Perfect Mind
In 1945 several pre-Christian scrolls were found near the town of Nag Hammadi, Egypt. Included in these texts was a Gnostic poem spoken by the divine power Sophia. We have so far been unable to trace a complete translation of this text, despite enquiries to the British Museum, but include here a part of it. In tone and feeling it is reminiscent of the Charge, which was almost certainly written by Gardner, a few years after 1945. Gardner, almost certainly, had contacts with the British Museum's department of Egyptology.

> I am the unlearned, and they can learn from me,
> I am knowledge, and I am ignorance,
> I am falsehood, and I am truth,
> I am shame, and I am boldness,
> I am shameless, and I am ashamed,
> I am the whore and the Holy one,
> I am the wife and the virgin.
> I am the ruler of my offspring, and my power is from him,

I am sinless, and the root of all sin derives from me,
Whatever I will happens to me,
I am compassionate and I am cruel.
I am the one who is praised and the one who is despised,
What you see outside you, you see inside you, it is invisible and it is your garment,
In my weakness do not forsake me, do not be afraid of my power,
I am control and the uncontrollable.
Do not be ignorant of me, be on your guard,
I am the one who is called justice, and I am gross iniquity,
I am the knowledge of my enquiry.
I am the one whom they call life, and the one whom you call death,
I am the judgement, and I am the acquittal.
I am the slave of him who prepared me,
Hear me, learn from my word,
You who know me, I am the union and the dissolution,
I am substance and the one who has no substance,
Do not be ignorant of me,
I am the one whose image is great, and I am the one who has no image.
Come forward to me and establish great ones amongst the small, come forward to childhood,
I am the one who cries out and I listen,
I am the knowledge of my name,
I am the first and the last,
I am the utterance of my name.

A Third Version of the Charge

I am the Moon shining on dark water. I am the reflection in a lightless room. I am that which is within you and can only be seen from inside. For my love, mountains have moved and the seas have lain still. I am the want in the mouths of the wealthy and I am the need in the hearts of the poor, I am the cruelty within the sunlight and rest in the light of the Moon. From times past I have been joy and sorrow, pain and healing, lust and innocence. In times to come I will be hope and futility, faith and despair. For I am that which lies inside and can only be seen from without, and I am that which is all around and can only be known from within. For in my life there is death and in my love there is knowledge. Know that to find me, you must cease looking, and to know me will be to find yourself.

So look again on the Moon of Hecate. So look again on the Moon of Ages. Look again at the light in the blackness. Look once more again at the self in unself and in the unself in self. And glory, revel, feast in the knowing of me.

SOLITARY DRAWING DOWN THE MOON

If you do not belong to a group or Coven, you do not have to miss out on Drawing Down the Moon. At the Full Moon you can perform a ritual of Moon worship and empowerment on your own. If you can do this outdoors, great. But do think of your personal safety, we would not recommend a woman to go out into the fields or woods on her own in this day and age. Yes, the Goddess does watch over her own, but she doesn't expect you to take unnecessary risks. If you do not have a secluded garden you may well be better off indoors.

If the night is clear, try to find a window where the moonlight shines in, in warm weather you may also like to open the window. If this is not possible use your normal working space. Prepare yourself as you would for any working. If at all possible, perform this ritual skyclad, Set up your altar on the window sill or any convenient surface where the moonlight can shine on it. In addition to the Elements you will also need the equipment for a self blessing.

You do not need to put up a circle or to summon the quarters. When you are ready, perform a Self Blessing. At the point where you say "Bless me mother, for I am thy child" open your eyes and gaze up at the Moon, remain kneeling and meditate on the Full Moon. If you wish you may also read the Charge in whatever version you prefer. But do not simply read it, think about the words you are saying and concentrate on their meaning. When you are ready clear up after yourself as usual and write up your experience in your Book of Shadows. Many people who live and work on their own like to indulge in 'Moonbathing', that is lying skyclad in the light of the full Moon whilst meditating.

Some guidelines on writing Rituals for group workings.

>Things to bear in mind:
>The Ritual must be appropriate for both the occasion and for the people who will attend.
>
>Do not try to cram too many things into a Ritual. Resist the temptation to be clever or to show off, remember to keep it simple. The Ritual should be unhurried, serious, and should flow; no hiccups or changes of direction.
>
>Unless the High Priestess and/or High Priest decides otherwise, there should be no audience; all group members should participate in the Ritual as equally as possible, guests should have some active part too. No-one should be asked to do something they are uncomfortable with, feel unable to do, or have an unfamiliar role sprung upon them. As far as possible, roles should be assigned in advance so people have time to prepare. Working group members should all be able to call Quarters, invite the Lord and Lady and cast the circle etc. without prior notice. Pieces of paper should be dispensed with as far as possible, roles and speeches should be learned.
>
>Altar and props should be prepared well in advance. Everything should be in place before people start to arrive. The Ritual should be explained at the start, to give everyone an indication of what is to happen, and what the relevance of each part is.

When you organise a Ritual, you are responsible for the way it goes. This means if others are uncertain or ill at ease, it is your responsibility to make them comfortable. If they feel left out or like a spare wheel, it is up to you to ensure they feel included. If you allow it to get out of hand or degenerate into a farce you are letting down yourself, your group and the Craft as a whole. If you would rather organise a party with a short theatrical in which you and your friends play the starring roles, then do that, do not use the Craft as an excuse.

Outline Ritual :

> Introduction – welcome, what the purpose is and what will happen
>
> Consecration and/or Blessing of Elements
>
> Calling of Quarters, or Guardians etc.
>
> Invite Lord and Lady.
>
> Cast Circle – for Closed workings, Esbats, not at Sabbats.
>
> Set the Scene – pathworking, banishing, or introductory piece.
>
> Power raising – chanting, dancing etc.
>
> The Ritual – Sabbats should reflect the turning of the Wheel of the Year, the current season and include a Rite which will reflect this in a way relevant to our lives.
>
> Full Moon – usually Closed unless extenuating circumstances. It is not necessary to Draw Down the Moon at every Esbat, only do this when there are suitable people in a suitable frame of mind. Scrying, healing, pathworking can all form a central part of the Esbat.

Other workings – ensure your motives and intentions are pure, do not use magic and Ritual at any and every set back or opportunity. Remember magic is a last resort and not a substitute for life. It must never be used on anyone else without their express consent.

Wine and cakes or Great Rite as appropriate – do not split a working couple when assigning these roles, and remember that, in the Great Rite, they are representing the Lord and Lady for the whole group.

Blessing – this can be seasonal, for a Sabbat, or general for other rituals.

Banish the Quarters.

Thank the Lord and Lady.

Close the circle (if used),

"Merry Meet, Merry Part, Merry Meet Again.
Blessed Be."

MAGIC

Magic is the ability to cause change in people, events, and things, by sheer control of will. There are many methods of making magic, for example:

>**SYMPATHETIC MAGIC** – the use of an object, named or labelled, to represent the person or thing which is intended to be changed, frequently used in healing. This is where the fith fath, a clay or wax doll, comes in.
>
>**INCANTATIONS** – the use of chants, rhymes or similar.
>
>**CORD MAGIC** – the use of coloured cords and knots.
>
>**CANDLE MAGIC** – using candles and oils.
>
>**TALISMANIC MAGIC** – the construction and empowerment of an object designed to be carried or worn.

These, and other, methods can be combined in a 'spell' or ritual to cause the desired effect. In this chapter we have included one example of candle magic and example of a ritual to produce an amulet of protection.

One of the most important things to remember is to *be careful what you wish for.* You should not work magic without careful consideration of the possible consequences. For example if you wish for money and quick, you may get it from the death of a loved one — far better to wish for the opportunity to earn money. Also bear in mind the principal of three-fold retribution; if what you do causes a negative effect, you will bear the negative effect three times over. There's also the question of the Wiccan Rede — Do what thou wilt an' it harm none. In addition, as has been said earlier, magic should not be used as a substitute for living; if you want to pass a test, study for it. By all means ask for more concentration, confidence, or inspiration but simply wishing to pass the test will not benefit you in the long run.

The next issue is whether to work magic for others. Most groups have a healing list, names of people who have asked, or whose near and dear have asked, for magic to be worked on their behalf. There will also be requests for other types of magic to be worked. All of these will usually be undertaken by the Coven. However, if you are considering working ritual on someone you must be careful not to alter their personality or psyche in a way they would not like. A good rule of thumb is not to work for others without their express consent.

In every case you should prepare yourself and set up the circle as usual, ensuring that you have all the things you will need on the altar. Where the construction of something lengthy is involved, for example a fith fath, you may start the process outside of the circle, but it must be completed within. Then, inside the circle, you go over the actions of making, in mime, to empower the object.

In order to ensure that the correct influences will operate you will need to refer to a table of correspondences. Cords, candles and altar cloth should be of the right colour, incenses and oils of the right scent and so forth. A short table is included at the end of this chapter for you to build upon.

A CANDLE SPELL TO INCREASE PSYCHIC AWARENESS
In order to maximise the influences in your favour, you will need to take into account the phase of the Moon, the day and the time. As the spell is designed to increase your psychic awareness, you will choose to work on the waxing (increasing) Moon, some time during the week before the full Moon. Consulting your table of correspondences you see that the Moon is the planet of Divination. Looking at your table of planetary hours you see that Monday is the day for the Moon and the hours are 1am, 8am, 3pm and 10pm. As you are not able to be uninterrupted until the evening, you time your ritual to commence at 10pm.

In addition to your usual preparations, you will need on your altar an unused candle of solid colour, some oil to anoint the candle, and your Boline, or a consecrated knife.

The correspondences for the Moon are:

Scents: Jasmine, Poppy and Myrtle.
The last two are difficult to get so you will use Jasmine as your oil. Essential oils are purer but expensive, a perfume oil will be sufficient.

Colours: Red.
You will need a candle of solid colour, unused and unscented. It does not need to be large.

Plants: Opium, Lotus, Mushroom, Seaweed and Watercress. If possible you will make your incense from these (missing out Opium). Alternatively you can buy ready made incense for the Moon or use commercially made incense sticks, cones or grains, in the appropriate fragrances. In this case you may be able to obtain Opium.

Having made the usual preparations and cast your circle in the prescribed manner, you are now ready to begin. If you are not using a Boline consecrate and bless the knife, remember, you do not use your Athame to cut! Use one of the methods for raising power, keeping your intention firmly in mind. When you are ready take your knife and inscribe into the candle the planetary sigil for the Moon, or carve a short version of your wish. Next, you anoint the candle with the oil, cover it thoroughly but be sparing in your use of the oil, don't swamp the thing. To anoint, you rub the candle from the centre to the ends, not from one end to the other. State your intent out aloud and light the candle. Remain and meditate on your purpose. The circle may now be removed, the quarters banished etc. The candle should be allowed to burn all the way down. If this is not possible, e.g. for safety reasons, as you should never leave a burning candle unattended, then snuff (do not blow) the candle out. Do not use the candle for any other purpose, Clear away, and don't forget to earth yourself and write it up.

RITUAL TO CONSECRATE AN AMULET OF PROTECTION
Occasionally you may be asked to provide someone with an object to protect them, or to bless something they already own for that purpose. In addition to all the usual things on your altar you will need the object to be consecrated. As this object has to be carried by the person in order for it to work, jewellery is the most common type of amulet.

Having consulted your tables of correspondences and planetary hours you find that Mars is the planet of defence. So you time your ritual for a Tuesday at 1am, 8am, 3pm or 10pm. Your altar cloth is Red and you are burning Pine incense. As an amulet you have chosen a Bloodstone set in silver. The Elements should be blessed and consecrated, the Quarters summoned, the Lord and Lady invited and the circle sealed. It is a good idea to commence with the Banishment of Unwanted Influences, to ensure that your focus will be pure.

Take the object in your right hand and perform the following:

> " I do bless and consecrate thee O creature of stone and silver, with Air (pass it through the incense smoke), I do consecrate and bless thee with Fire (pass it quickly through the candle flame), I do consecrate and bless thee with Water (sprinkle a little water on it), and I do consecrate and bless thee with Earth (sprinkle a little salt on the object), to cleanse thee of all impurities."

Place the object on your Altar pentacle, take your Athame and draw an Earth pentacle over the object and say "By the power invested in me .... (your name) as Priest(ess) I do command thee to be an amulet of protection for .... (use the name of the person for whom the amulet is intended), at all times and in all places". As you are drawing the pentacle visualise an electric blue light leaving the end of your Athame and entering into the object. "As is my will so mote it be. Blessed Be."

Then wrap the amulet in a piece of new paper or cloth so that no-one may come into contact with it until it reaches the person for whom it is intended.

Banish the quarters, thank the Lord and Lady, take down the circle, clear up, ground yourself and write up the ritual taking especial care to note the date and time.

The Amulet should be given to its intended owner as soon as practical; they should wear it or carry it at all times. They should not clean it. That is not to say that it cannot get wet, but that it should not be intentionally cleaned as this will remove the energy you have so carefully imbued it with. Of course a hand-made amulet, created in the circle, is a much stronger form of the same. By putting your energies into the creation of anything you empower it.

PLANETARY HOURS

The use of Planetary hours is not essential, but by doing so you will help to maximise the external forces in your favour. Whenever possible, time your ritual to start at the correct planetary hour on the right day to maximise the planetary influences. Of course you should also observe the correct phase of the Moon. This does not apply when you are timing ritual to coincide with a particular event.

The planetary influences can be found by looking at the Table of Correspondences later in this book.

Table of Planetary Hours

Day	Monday	Tuesday	Wednesday
Planet for day	Moon	Mars	Mercury
am			
1	Moon	Mars	Mercury
2	Saturn	Sun	Moon
3	Jupiter	Venus	Saturn
4	Mars	Mercury	Jupiter
5	Sun	Moon	Mars
6	Venus	Saturn	Sun
7	Mercury	Jupiter	Venus
8	Moon	Mars	Mercury
9	Saturn	Sun	Moon
10	Jupiter	Venus	Saturn
11	Mars	Mercury	Jupiter
12	Sun	Moon	Mars
p.m.			
13	Venus	Saturn	Sun
14	Mercury	Jupiter	Venus
15	Moon	Mars	Mercury
16	Saturn	Sun	Moon
17	Jupiter	Venus	Saturn
18	Mars	Mercury	Jupiter
19	Sun	Moon	Mars
20	Venus	Saturn	Sun
21	Mercury	Jupiter	Venus
22	Moon	Mars	Mercury
23	Saturn	Sun	Moon
24	Jupiter	Venus	Saturn

Table of Planetary Hours

Day	Thursday	Friday	Saturday	Sunday
Planet for day	Jupiter	Venus	Saturn	Sun
am				
1	Jupiter	Venus	Saturn	Sun
2	Mars	Mercury	Jupiter	Venus
3	Sun	Moon	Mars	Mercury
4	Venus	Saturn	Sun	Moon
5	Mercury	Jupiter	Venus	Saturn
6	Moon	Mars	Mercury	Jupiter
7	Saturn	Sun	Moon	Mars
8	Jupiter	Venus	Saturn	Sun
9	Mars	Mercury	Jupiter	Venus
10	Sun	Moon	Mars	Mercury
11	Venus	Saturn	Sun	Moon
12	Mercury	Jupiter	Venus	Saturn
p.m.				
13	Moon	Mars	Mercury	Jupiter
14	Saturn	Sun	Moon	Mars
15	Jupiter	Venus	Saturn	Sun
16	Mars	Mercury	Jupiter	Venus
17	Sun	Moon	Mars	Mercury
18	Venus	Saturn	Sun	Moon
19	Mercury	Jupiter	Venus	Saturn
20	Moon	Mars	Mercury	Jupiter
21	Saturn	Sun	Moon	Mars
22	Jupiter	Venus	Saturn	Sun
23	Mars	Mercury	Jupiter	Venus
24	Sun	Moon	Mars	Mercury

Table of Correspondences

Day	Monday	Tuesday	Wednesday
Planet	Moon	Mars	Mercury
Colour(s)	White - new Red - full Black - dk of	Red	Violet Indigo
Scent(s)	Jasmine Poppy Myrtle	Pine Tobacco Cypress	Storax Mace Sandalwood
Attributions	Dreams Female fertility Illusion Divination	Defence Discord Battle Attack Severity	Travel Business Knowledge Exams
Element	Water	Fire	Water/air
Metal	Silver	Iron	Mercury
Jewels	Moonstone Quartz	Bloodstone Ruby Garnet	Opal Agate
Animal(s)	Cat Hare	Basilisk	Jackal Twin-serpents

Table of Correspondences

Day	Thursday	Friday	Saturday	Sunday
Planet	Jupiter	Venus	Saturn	Sun
Colour(s)	Purple Blue	Green Rose	Black Dark blue	Gold Yellow
Scent(s)	Cedar Nutmeg	Benzion Jasmine Rose	Civet Myrrh Cinnamon	Frankincense Laurel
Attributions	Wealth Lust Ambition Career Male fertility	Romance Friends Beauty Self respect Pleasure	Study Title Position Binding Banishing	Honour Power Glory Money Work
Element	Air/Fire	Water/earth	Earth/water	Fire/air
Metal	Tin	Copper	Lead	Gold
Jewels	Amethyst Sapphire Chrysolite	Amber Emerald	Pearl Onyx Sapphire	Topaz Yellow/ diamond
Animal(s)	Unicorn	Dove	Crow Raven	Eagle Lion Phoenix

Table of Correspondences			
Day	**Monday**	**Tuesday**	**Wednesday**
Plants	Opium Lotus Mushroom Seaweed Watercress	Chiles Ginger Garlic Mustard Basil Gentia	Caraway Dill Fennel Lavender Mandrake Horehound
Chakra	Svadisthana	Manipura	Vissudha
Goddesses *examples*	*New* Artemis Nimue *Full* Diana Mari *Waning* Hecate Nanna *Misc.* Lunah Sellene Hathor Isis	Anath Morrigan	Athena Maat Metis
Gods *examples*	Khonsu Sin Ganesha	Ares Mars Nergal	Hermes Mercury Nebo Thoth

Table of Correspondences

Day	Thursday	Friday	Saturday	Sunday
Plants	Anise Clover Mint Balm Oak Olive	Almond Apple Fig Rose Elder Geranium	Aconite Marijuana Hemlock Cypress Yew Thyme	Citrus Saffron Marigold Birch Acacia Ash
Chakra		Anahata/ Svadisthana	Vissudha/ Muladara	Anahata
Goddesses *examples*	Isis Hera Juno Themis	Aphrodite Venus Ishtar Hathor Inanna Freya Beltis Mari Astarte	Isis Hera Kali Nepthys Rhea Demeter Bhavani	Amaterasu Bast Ilat Theia Sekhmet
Gods *examples*	Zeus Thor Marduk Jupiter Woden Lugh	Eros Adonis	Cronos Saturn Adar	Helios Hyperion Ra Utu Krishna Rama

THE WITCH WITHIN

So, we have seen that Witches follow the Cycle of the Moon, Celebrate the Sabbats, Worship the God and the Goddess. They hold rituals, work magic, scry and divine, and develop latent psychic powers. But how do they actually do it?

Most people have a measure of psychic power which, as we have said, is usually suppressed by early training. Often described as the sixth sense, it can only be rediscovered and developed if the other five senses are used to the full. Strange though it may seem, you need to learn to see, hear, smell, taste and touch properly before you can really start to develop your psychic ability. In addition, you will have to learn to understand and use your mind, and to trust your instincts.

In previous chapters we have talked about aspects of the God and the Goddess, the Elements, the Moon and the Wheel of the Year, and how we can relate these to ourselves. In this chapter we have included exercises for self development and exercises to help us refine the use of our senses. These, taken together with the exercises and pathworkings found elsewhere in the book will enable the newcomer to explore themselves and the world around them more fully, whether they decide that the Craft is for them or not.

Firstly, our senses: sight, hearing, taste, touch and smell.

> **SIGHT** – "But I know how to see!" you say. Well do you? Do you use your mind when you see? Try the following, sometimes known as Kim's game. Get a friend to take a tray and a number of objects, say twenty. Look at the tray and the objects for one minute. Your friend then covers the tray and you list the objects. Try it a second time, but this time your friend moves an object, takes one away and adds another, all without you seeing. Did you get it correct? Good, now try it with a shelf of books or a room full of furniture. It's quite hard, mainly because we take for granted what we see, our

imagination will fill in any blank spots if necessary. But visualisation is one of the most important tools of the Witch and if we do not see accurately how will we visualise, if we do not see clearly in the here and now how will we develop clairvoyance (clear sight) on a mental level? Try another exercise; watch people you cannot hear, e.g. through a window, consider their feelings, are they happy, sad, tired, alert? How much can you learn about them using only your eyes? What makes this so interesting is the fact that, for most of us, sight is the primary sense used. In the following four exercises sight is shut off in order to concentrate on the other senses.

HEARING – In a room on your own find a comfortable chair, sit down and blindfold yourself. Now listen, listen carefully. Think about what you hear, let your mind develop a picture of what you are hearing. Then remove the blindfold and go and check. Was your mental picture accurate? Try this outside in the park (just close your eyes, don't use a blindfold), compare what you hear with your eyes open with what you hear with them closed. You should find that, at first, you hear more with your eyes shut.

TOUCH – This time try to differentiate objects by touch alone, again, it is useful to get a friend to help you. Don't just stop at trying to work out what something is, can you tell what colour it is? Alternatively, blindfold yourself and take a *careful* tour of a room or your house. Examine things with your fingers, note the textures, whether they are warm or cool to the touch, are they friendly or unfriendly? What is your overall impression of the room?

TASTE – Take a selection of foods and taste them blindfold. Try small quantities on different areas of your tongue. Note the differences. Note the different feelings and memories that taste can evoke. Most of us eat without really tasting, that is why so many of our foods contain flavour enhancers such as salt, herbs, monosodium glutamate etc. Taste and smell are linked, so if you can gently plug your nostrils try tasting things you cannot smell.

SMELL – Another blindfold test, teach yourself to differentiate herbs, spices and flowers by smell. Again, don't just stop at identifying, what thoughts, feelings and memories are evoked by different scents? Use taste and smell together, learn to smell as the cat does; whilst breathing in through your nose, let some of the air enter in through your mouth, directing it across the roof of your mouth. This takes a bit of practice but, when you can do it, you'll find that your repertoire of smells is enhanced, you'll also find it easier to detect a good wine by scent rather than finding out when it's halfway to your stomach!

Exercising your instinct is somewhat harder. Learning one of the forms of divination and keeping a divination diary, a record of your readings, is one way. But you can also practise on a daily basis. Look at the people around you, especially those you don't know. Try to predict their actions and movements. Try looking at people outside your window, who will be first to cross the road, change their bag from one hand to the other? Don't worry if at first you're not too good at it, concentrate on the right 'guesses' until you come to know that your intuition is correct. By the way, most of us actually use this skill quite unconsciously, but when we get it right, we call it coincidence.

Practise these skills on a daily basis and you'll find that your appreciation of the world is greatly enhanced. You will see colours and shapes in a different way, scents and tastes will be clearer. You will also find that your dreams are more vivid and your visualisations more graphic, and hence your working more powerful.

However, that still leaves the hardest part; self knowledge, self understanding and self integration. The starting points of self control, without which we cannot hope to control anything else. In the Craft the power of the mind is essential and for that you need control of the mind. Think back to the physics you did at school. At its simplest; matter is not solid, everything is made of atoms comprised of elements which spin and vibrate at different frequencies. So everything vibrates at its own frequency or vibrationary level. To work magic we must tune into these frequencies. We must know and feel these vibrationary levels and be able to link with, and alter, them. If we do not understand our own 'frequencies' we cannot hope to succeed. One of the key notes of the Craft is "Know Thyself". Remember the Charge "If that which thou seekest......". Working in and with the Craft will bring a greater understanding of self, but a lot of work has to be done by the individual towards this end. This is not an easy path and, generally, is not a path with an end.

We each of us have a variety of qualities, feelings and emotions. There are aspects of ourselves which give us pleasure and of which we are proud, and there are other aspects with which we are not so happy. We refer here to basic personality traits, not just bad habits. Most of us waste a lot of mental energy trying to hide or conceal those things which we dislike about ourselves, when we would be better off trying to understand and integrate the darker aspects into the whole. That is not to say that you should give in to antisocial impulses and actions, but rather that by knowing why, for instance, you want to kick every dog you meet, you can control the desire to do so. Very often the process of self understanding means re-evaluating early conditioning. You may have been brought up that anger is wrong, when in fact it is the inappropriate expression of anger which is wrong. Hence you must understand exactly what angers you in order to react in the appropriate way.

Dealing appropriately with your feelings and reactions can only come about when you understand your deepest feelings and inner motivations. The process of self examination is something all of us do to a greater or lesser extent, but mostly we forget the cardinal rules:

Be kind to your self; you are a nice person, treat yourself as such. Self examination does not mean mentally beating yourself black and blue for the human actions and reactions of the past. Try to understand without being self critical. Every time you make a list of 'faults' balance it with a list of good points.

Be honest with yourself; about yourself and about other influences in your life. Do you enjoy practical jokes because you have a good sense of humour, because you enjoy manipulating people or because this was the only way your parents showed affection towards you?

Be forgiving; of others and of yourself. We all make mistakes, sometimes bad ones. You may never be able to forget, but you can forgive.

The following exercises are designed to help you start your journey of self understanding. They have been used by the authors in the Coven setting and, with real effort, prove extremely valuable. All of the exercises are for you alone, so keep them away from prying eyes. In almost every case you will need to go back to them time and time again, probably over a period of a few months. So there's no excuse in saying you don't have time, just do a little now and then.

Firstly, write a list of one hundred things you enjoy doing. Big things and little things. Use this list, when you feel low get it out and go and do one. Treat yourself, whether it's a walk in the country or just a hot bath. Give yourself a break, you've earned it. Now, on to the hard work.

Write a list of one hundred things you do well. Yes, it is possible, there are a hundred. Start with little things; cooking toast, walking the dog, anything so long as you start.

Write a list of things you dislike about yourself (most people find this bit easy), but every time you write a dislike, write something you like about yourself (not such a pushover now?). Review the dislikes and see how many you can turn into positives. For example, queuing at the supermarket checkout drives you nuts — you dislike wasting time.

Examine yourself naked in the mirror, write a list of at least twenty things you like about your body.

Write out the story of an episode in your past which you regret. Then read it as though it were written by a very dear friend. Examine it charitably and kindly. Then rewrite it giving yourself the kindness you would give a friend. When you are ready, take both copies and burn them, or shred them and bury them. Tell yourself that this episode has gone, and mean it, whilst you may never forget, you can now put it aside and go forward. Don't worry if you are not ready to destroy it immediately, put it away in a safe place until you are ready.

We mentioned vibrations and frequencies a little earlier. You should also practise working with vibrationary levels. A safe method of practise is to work with the Elements and the Guardians, especially when summoning the Quarters. This can be done in many ways but sound is probably the easiest to start with. If you close your eyes and experiment with vocalising the name of a Guardian, you should find you start to see a colour behind your eyelids. When this colour matches that of the quarter you have the right resonance for that Guardian, e.g. Michael – red. When you are fully linked with the vibrationary level for Michael you will also start to feel heat and smell the scents of summer. For Michael is the Guardian of the South the point of Fire which corresponds with the season of summer. Work through all the quarters until you do not have to strive to achieve the correct resonance, it comes naturally.

Then move on to other exercises of 'mind power'. If you have a pet try 'tuning in' to it so that you can call it to you without sound. Concentrate on the name of a friend and will them to contact you. Take care with the latter, you don't want to treat your friends as laboratory animals. In all these exercises don't forget to write them up in your Book of Shadows.

Now, just because self development is necessary, it does not mean that you have to have perfected yourself to be a Witch. No Witch we have ever met is anything like perfect. It does, however, mean that we strive for greater understanding and wisdom through the Craft.

PATHWORKING AND GUIDED MEDITATION

In this chapter we intend to give an introduction to Pathworking and Guided Meditation, but first let us define what we mean by the terms:

> **MEDITATION** – the focusing of the mind onto a single object (such as a candle flame), word or mantra (simple chant), in order to control all conscious thought.
>
> **GUIDED MEDITATION** – where a story is followed to the exclusion of all other conscious thought.
>
> **PATHWORKING** – different to guided meditation in that, at some point of the story, the listener is encouraged to ask a question or listen to a 'voice' or make a choice. The answer thus received is thought to be derived from the subconscious mind, or from the God or Goddess within.

We have included in this chapter a Pathworking to the God Pan and Pathworkings to each of the elements. The Pathworking to the Element of Water has also been included in guided meditation form in order that readers may see for themselves an example of the differences between the two techniques. A Pathworking to the Triple Goddess can be found in the chapter on the God and the Goddess. All the Pathworkings included here were written by the authors and designed for group use, all were prefaced and concluded using the "Relaxation Technique" which is also included. The Element Pathworkings were originally used as part of Elemental rituals within a closed circle, but can be safely used by any group which follows the basic guidelines. A complete Element ritual has been included in the chapter on the Elements. In all cases it has been assumed that one person acts as 'reader', guidelines for this person are enclosed in brackets. Where such an instruction appears saying (PAUSE) it is useful to count slowly to twenty under the breath, in order to give the participants time to accomplish whatever is expected of them.

In all relaxation, meditation or Pathworking sessions the first thing to do is to create the right atmosphere. Whilst it is possible for accomplished meditators to achieve a state of altered consciousness almost at will, those with less experience will get more out of it if they start in the right surroundings. The idea is to remove as many distractions as possible. Shut any pets and non-participants out, switch off the telephone. The room should be comfortably warm, with low lighting. People should have enough space, not be packed like sardines. If they are to lie down they may be more comfortable if they bring a rug or blanket for the purpose, this can also be used by 'chilly mortals' to wrap themselves up in. Sometimes it is a good idea to play some soothing music at a low level as this helps to screen out any external noises, and incense can also be used to create the mood.

The participants should be prepared. Whilst this can be an enjoyable experience, it should still be approached seriously. This is not to be undertaken by anyone who is ill or taking drugs (legal or otherwise), nor by anyone who has had a few drinks. It is very important that participants stay with the story line. They should not leave the path, as it is possible to get lost and be unable to find their way back to the here and now completely. It is a good idea to summarise the story line before beginning, you never know if someone has a hidden fear or phobia which may be triggered during the tale.

The reader should be aware of the technique for bringing someone back who seems to be experiencing distress, or who has drifted off to sleep. The latter is not an indictment against either the reader or the sleeper, it simply means they have relaxed more fully than intended. Their subconscious will have picked up on the session even if their conscious is not aware of it. This means that the reader should position themselves so that they can observe and, if necessary, reach all the individuals in the room.

So firstly, how to bring someone back: If during a session you see someone appearing distressed (they tend to look like a sleeper having a nightmare), or if someone does not return from the relaxation at the end, the reader should approach this person, and wake them by touching them gently on the arm and calling their name. Have a smiling and reassuring expression on your face when you do it. Imagine you are waking a young child from a bad dream and you can't go far wrong. In any event don't rush in to do this at the end of the relaxation as some people simply take longer than others to shake off the relaxation.

So you have your room prepared and your group together. Give them a few moments to leave behind what they were doing before they arrived, let them greet each other, check no one needs the bathroom and that everyone has put out their cigarettes. Outline the story to them and settle them down.

Throughout the relaxation and Pathworking the reader should use a gentle relaxed voice, and should take their time. Whilst you don't want a monotone, try to avoid sudden or dramatic changes in pitch or volume. Don't rush it, many readers find that they are able to establish the tempo during the breathing part of the relaxation technique, by watching the participants and keying in to the speed of their breathing. It is important during this stage that you don't count aloud, one, two, three, four but rather that you let the group set their own pace. Try to avoid rustling your script and make sure beforehand that you have a glass of water to hand, as you'll need it if you don't!

RELAXATION TECHNIQUE:
Welcome, settle yourselves comfortably, uncross your arms and legs and close your eyes. We are going to start with relaxing our bodies so that our minds may concentrate on the Pathworking.

What I am going to do to is to ask you to feel each part of your body and as I mention it, to move that part very gently:

Think about and gently move your toes and your feet, gently stretch and rotate your ankles, tighten and relax the muscles in your calves, gently move your knees, tighten and relax your thighs. Draw in your tummy and then push it all the way out, let it relax. Take a deep breath in through your nose, hold the breath, then push the air all the way out, breath normally again. Wriggle and move your shoulders, tighten and relax the muscles in your upper arms, gently move your elbows, tighten and relax the muscles in your lower arms, rotate your wrists. Make a tight fist with each of your hands, then let it go and relax. Stretch and rotate your neck and head. Screw your face up as much as you can, feel all your face muscles and then relax.

Relax and breathe normally, feel the weight of your body being supported and held, let your muscles relax and let the floor take your weight.

You are listening to the sound of my voice and all outside sounds and distractions will start to fade away. You know that, if at any time you experience anything you do not like you will be able to open your eyes and sit up. You will be totally relaxed and ready to deal with any eventuality.

I want you to think now about your breathing. Breath in through your nose and out through your mouth, feel your chest rise, then as your diaphragm expands feel your tummy rise. Hold each breath for the count of four. Slowly release your breath through your mouth to the count of four. Breath in to the count of four, hold for four, breath out to the count of four.

Breathe in for four, hold the breath for four, breathe out for four.

Remember to breath in through your nose and out through your mouth, breathe in for four, hold the breath for four, breathe out for four. Feel the air passing in through your nose passing over the back of your throat and down into your lungs. Hold it there for the count of four. Feel the air passing up from your lungs into your mouth and out of your body. Breathe in for four, hold the breath for four, breathe out for four. Feel the good fresh air passing in, feel the stale used air going out. Breathe in for four, hold the breath for four, breathe out for four.

Think of the new air going in as a golden light, each breath taking it deeper into your body; filling your lungs and your chest, feel the golden light filling your stomach and relaxing you. Feel the golden light passing down into your legs and feet, relaxing you and calming you. Feel the light passing down your arms and into your hands, driving all the cares and worries away. Feel it rising up your neck and into your head, filling you with peace and calm. Breathe in for four, hold the breath for four, breathe out for four. Your body is being filled with golden cleansing light.

(At this stage you read the Pathworking or meditation that has been selected, being careful to observe the participants and to bring everyone out of the path by reversing the route by which they entered the story.)

You are returning to the here and now, and you start to be aware once more of this room and the people in it. You are aware of the other sounds around you. You can feel again the weight of your body relaxed against the floor. When you are ready you will open your eyes, take your time and open your eyes to return to us now.

Move and gently shake your feet and legs, your arms and hands. Take a few deep breaths and look around you. When you are ready clap your hands and gently stamp you feet.

(When everyone appears alert, speak to and get a response from each of them. This ensures that they really have returned to the here and now. Ask them how they feel. At this stage it is a good idea to serve a hot drink and to get people to discuss their experiences from the session. If someone is hesitant do not force them to say what they saw or felt in front of the group, ask them to come back to you later alone.)

AIR ELEMENT PATHWORKING:
You are walking slowly through the hills. The sun is shining and the sky is a clear blue. The air is clean and crisp. The

grass underfoot is green and soft, as you walk you notice tiny flowers. Ahead of you the high peaks of the mountains rise up towards the sky. The air is enlivening and you feel strong and confident. You know that nothing and no-one can harm you.

The ground ahead of you starts to rise and you let your steps follow the rise of the land. Although you are climbing you feel no effort or strain. As you climb the air becomes colder and crisper. The grass and flowers give way to rocks and the track you are following becomes steeper. Still you are calm and relaxed and you climb upwards easily.

The track twists and weaves between ever larger rocks and boulders and yet you continue. Below you, you can see the land stretching out into the distance. The track becomes steeper still and you are now climbing in earnest, using your hands to gain hold on the rocks to help you continue on upwards. The air is cooler here and you can feel the wind plucking at your clothes.

Eventually you are at the top. You are pleased that you have achieved the climb so well. You see in front of you one last boulder and the track goes around it to the left. You follow the track and it brings you out onto a wide ledge. There below you it seems the world is spread out like a patchwork quilt.

Perched on a branch on the ledge is a giant eagle. The bird towers above you. Its plumage is a blend of golds and browns. Its great talons grip the branch as it regards you with a great golden eye. Although awesome, the bird is not frightening and you feel calm and confident in it's gaze. The eagle speaks to you and tells you that today it will grant you a special favour. Today you will be transformed into an eagle too and you will fly and feel the currents and strength of the air.

The bird bids you to sit down and close your eyes. So you sit on the ledge and allow your eyes to shut. Around you, you seem to hear a great whirring, the sound of wings in the wind. When you open your eyes the eagle is still there and you feel a great companionship with the great bird. You look down at yourself and see that you too have tawny brown plumage, great wings and talons on your feet.

Together you and the great bird stand and spread your wings. Moving them even gently you are aware of your great power and strength. The bird looks at you again with his great golden eyes and together you take to the air. Flying feels totally natural to you and you find you can move effortlessly through the air. You can feel the wind passing through your plumage. Gliding, you allow the winds to take you and you can feel the warm air currents take you higher into the air, until the ledge where you started is far below you.

Together you and the great eagle swoop down the mountain side towards the land below. The air rushes past you cold and fresh. You can feel the way it supports your weight and yet allows you total freedom of movement. Soon you are swooping at the level of the treetops and beneath you, you can see the smaller birds and animals take cover. With your eagle's sight you can see the smallest movement in the trees or on the ground beneath you.

You fly on over the forest needing only the tiniest movement of your wings to keep the momentum going. Relax and enjoy your flight, store up the feelings of the wind and air and of effortless flight. Store up the sights and sounds of your passing over the forest and landscape as you and your companion fly onwards. (pause . . .)

Soon the landscape beneath you changes from forest to the plains, and you are now flying high over the farmlands laid out below you. You can see the patchwork of fields and the farm workers beneath you. One or two look up in awe as your great shadows pass over them. And still you fly on, enjoying the feeling of your wings carrying you and the air supporting you.

Again the landscape changes and you are heading out over rolling sandy dunes towards the great sea. You are aware of the change in the taste and feel of the air. A new saltiness, cooler buffeting winds encouraging you to rise and swoop, first high then low over the waves. The seas darken, and the waves become bigger as the winds rise. You are flying in the storm and you can feel now the power of the winds and the air. You are still calm and confident as you can feel your own strength is superior to that of the storm, and so you fly on enjoying the feeling of power over the elements. Enjoy and remember these feelings. (pause . . .)

The storm passes and once again the sky is blue, the seas are calm. You fly onwards towards the east where the Elementals and Guardians of Air are found. You can see clearly the form and nature of these people. (pause . . .) Let yourself travel to and meet with these people. (pause . . .). (You can either allow the group to envisage their own forms or you can describe forms such as Sylphs for them.)

You have covered vast miles, but do not feel tired, but exhilarated. Ahead of you once again is the land and now, leading the way you fly confidently on towards it. Once again you retrace your flight over the plain and over the forest. You fly onwards towards the mountain top where you started out. Reaching the ledge you and the great eagle land once more and folding your wings you can feel the way in which your plumage fits together perfectly. You once more close your eyes.

Now your thoughts move inwards on yourself, the resting form on the ledge. Feel within your self the qualities of air. The power and the subtlety of your thoughts. (pause . . .) The emotions and feelings that relate to the Air Element within you. (pause . . .) (Again you can give the group keywords if you wish or you can let them do the work themselves.)

When you open them the great bird has gone and you have resumed your human form. On your lap is a single tawny golden feather to remind you of your flight. Rising to your feet you take the feather and begin again your journey down the mountain.

(Talk them back through the ingoing journey. And finish with the closing portion of the Relaxation Technique.)

FIRE ELEMENT PATHWORKING:

You are resting in an old kitchen. The only light comes from a great open fire beside you. The light flickers and casts shadows and shapes on the walls and ceiling, which is beamed with rafters. The fire is fuelled with scented woods and burns fiercely, the room is filled with the crackling sounds of the fire, no other sound intrudes. The heat from the fire warms you and relaxes you.

You let your thoughts be drawn by the fire. The flames are red and black, orange and yellow, green and blue. Sparks fly and shapes shift. Your mind is drawn deeper by the fire. As you gaze into the flames you start to see and feel images of fire.

The pure fire of the volcano, molten rocks burning and flowing, great rivers of fire sweeping over the landscape, a fire nothing can halt or turn, watch and feel the power of fire to change. (short pause . . .)

The consuming flames of forest fire, hungry, thrusting, greedy, ravaging, destroying all in their path, watch and feel the fear of fire. (short pause . . .)

The flames of the bonfire, controlled and smoky, cleansing and purifying, ridding the earth of waste, watch and feel the cleanliness of fire. (short pause . . .)

The baking wastes of the desert at noon, the sun blazing overhead, the total absence of water and of life, the dry mouth and the burning skin, watch and feel death in fire. (short pause . . .)

The gentle morning sun, whispering over the land, rousing life in tree and flower, warming and waking the beasts and birds, watch and feel the welcome life of fire. (short pause . . .)

The pure and gentle light of the candle flame, dancing and shifting, lighting the dark, throwing shadows and pictures on the walls, as you gaze into the candle flame feel yourself drawn into it so that you too dance and shift, shimmer and illuminate. (short pause . . .)

Now the images in the fire shift and change, taking you on a journey towards the south where the Elementals and Guardians of Fire are found. You can see clearly the form and nature of these people. (pause . . .) Let yourself travel to and meet with these people. (pause . . .) (You can either allow the group to envisage their own forms or you can describe forms such as Salamanders for them.)

Now your thoughts move inwards on yourself, the resting form by the fire. Feel within your self the qualities of fire. The power and the strength of your passions. Their ability to change your life and your need to harness that energy. The emotions and feelings that relate to the Fire Element within you. (pause . . .). (Again you can give the group keywords if you wish or you can let them do the work themselves.)

Return now to your seat in the kitchen by the fire, feel the warmth and relax

(Talk them back through the ingoing journey. And finish with the closing portion of the Relaxation Technique.)

WATER ELEMENT PATHWORKING:

You are lying on a beautiful golden beach, above you the sky is a clear and deep blue, the sun is warm, the sand beneath you supports you and forms itself to your body. You are wearing light beach clothes and your feet are bare. You can feel the sun against your skin, warming you. There is a gentle breeze fanning your skin. You can hear the sound of the waves lapping against the beach, a gentle, lulling sound. You feel safe and secure, you know you are alone and nothing and no-one can hurt you. Over the sound of the surf you can hear the gentle call of the gulls. Behind you the sound of the breeze rustling the leaves in the trees. You lie for a while, enjoying the warmth of the sun, the gentle breeze and the sounds of the beach.

After a little while you sit up, stretch yourself and look around you. The beach is completely deserted, the sand golden, the sky blue and there is not a cloud to be seen. Higher up the beach you see a line of palm trees waving gently in the breeze, the green of their leaves highlighting the blue of the sky. Over the water a few gulls circle and call to one another. Beneath your hands you feel the soft, warm sand. Against your skin you feel the warm sun and the gentle breeze. You stand up and begin to walk down the waterline. You feel calm and at peace with the world. As you walk you enjoy the warmth of the sun and the feel of the sand beneath your feet. The gentle breeze caresses you skin. You notice tiny shells in the sand and the foam that each departing wave leaves behind sinks gently into the sand. Your steps take you into the edge of the water which is cooling on your feet, although still warm enough to be comfortable. The fresh sea air smells good and you fill your lungs, feeling the tranquillity and calm of the air and the sea. You walk further into the waves until they are lapping at your knees. As you gaze into the water around your legs, you notice the beautiful colours of the shells in the sand and the way the sunlight highlights first one colour, then another. In the water, tiny, brightly coloured fishes dart away from your approach. You continue walking, knee deep in the water, along the edge of the beach. The warm sunlight filling you with health and a sense of well-being. You are calm and relaxed, knowing that no harm can come to you.

As you gaze out across the waves you see larger fishes jumping and dancing in the water. You stop still and concentrate on what you are seeing. As your eyes come into focus you realise that you are watching a school of dolphins playing in the water. They are joyful and playful. As you stand watching you realise that a few of them are coming closer. There are two, maybe three dolphins dancing and playing quite near to you. You can hear their chirrups and clicks as they talk to each other.

One of them comes quite close and you can see the sunlight glistening on her wet skin, the water frothing as she frolics. Realising they mean you no harm you wade deeper into the water until it reaches your waist. The dolphin swims slowly up to you, until you can reach out and touch her. She feels smooth and warm to the touch, as she rolls back in the water you stroke her chin and belly and the trust she shows in you brings you feelings of greater confidence. The sun is still warm above you and the sand is only a few steps away, knowing you can move away whenever you wish, you decide to stay awhile with the dolphins. The confidence of the one dolphin brings the other two nearer, and soon they are swimming and playing near enough for you to touch.

You decide to enter the clear, clean water and swim and play with them. Soon you are swimming freely with them, you hold onto the fin of one of the dolphins and let her tow you through the water. You feel the warm water passing over your skin and the freedom of moving without effort. As she takes you diving deep under the water you realise that you can breath under water. You are totally relaxed and happy knowing that no harm can come to you.

The dolphin takes you deeper under the waves. The water is crystal clear and you realise that you can see a great distance, down to the sea bed. You stay awhile swimming and moving with the water enjoying being at one with the element. (pause . . .)

As you let the dolphin guide you, you realise that it is taking you on a journey towards the west where the Elementals and Guardians of Water are found. you can see clearly the form and nature of these people. (pause . . .) Let yourself travel to and meet with these people. (pause . . .) (You can either allow the group to envisage their own forms or you can describe forms such as undines for them.)

Once again your dolphin guide is beside you. Taking the fin of the dolphin you swim away and return to the surface of the water. The other dolphins are gone as your guide takes you close to the waters edge.

You become aware once more of the warmth of the sun and the refreshing cool of the water. You wade slowly through the water back to the beach. Once again you enjoy the feeling of the sand beneath your feet and the warm light breeze against your skin. Already you are being dried by the sun and the air. Once again the only sounds are the lapping of the waves and the cries of the gulls. You make your way to the edge of the sand and lie down in the shade of a tree. You close your eyes and rest, safe in the arms of the world around you.

Now your thoughts move inwards on yourself. Feel within your self the qualities of Water. Your emotions and the way they ebb and flow through your life. (pause . . .) The emotions and feelings that relate to the Water Element within you. (pause . . .) (Again you can give the group keywords if you wish or you can let them do the work themselves.)

(Talk them back through the ingoing journey. And finish with the closing portion of the Relaxation Technique.)

EARTH ELEMENT PATHWORKING:

You are lying in a newly ploughed field. The earth beneath you is rich and vibrant with life. You can smell the rich earthiness all around you. Feel the solidity of the ground supporting you without being hard. Become aware of the life in the very soil, of your companionship and kinship with it. As you lie there you feel yourself becoming at one with the earth.

Your flesh is as the soil itself, your bones are the hard rocks at the core of the earth, your blood is the streams and rivers flowing within the land. Your thoughts are as the crystals and gems of the land. Feel your heartbeat slow to the ancient pulse of the land. The seasons are as flickering lights passing quickly over your sight. Thousands of years have you lived and will yet live. You have seen the whole pageant of history pass and you continue on undisturbed. Feel the life of the land as your own life. You are the earth and yet of the earth. The earth moves within you and you within it. Your senses extend over vast miles to encompass the planet itself and you are aware of each and every part. Let your thoughts roam and feel your outermost limits. (pause . . .)

Now you travel to the north, where the Elementals and Guardians of Earth are found. You can see clearly the form and nature of these people. (pause . . .) Let your self travel to and meet with these people. (pause . . .) (You can either allow the group to envisage their own forms or you can describe forms such as Gnomes for them.)

Now your thoughts move back to the resting form in the field. Feel within your self the qualities of Earth. The substance of your body. (pause . . .) The emotions and feelings that relate to the Earth Element within you. (pause . . .) (Again you can give the group keywords if you wish or you can let them do the work themselves.)

(Talk them back through the ingoing journey. And finish with the closing portion of the Relaxation Technique.)

WATER ELEMENT GUIDED MEDITATION:
You are lying on a beautiful golden beach, above you the sky is a clear and deep blue, the sun is warm, the sand beneath you supports you and forms itself to your body. You are wearing light beach clothes and your feet are bare. You can feel the sun against your skin, warming you. There is a gentle breeze fanning your skin. You can hear the sound of the waves lapping against the beach, a gentle, lulling sound. You feel safe and secure, you know you are alone and nothing and no-one can hurt you. Over the sound of the surf you can hear the gentle call of the gulls. Behind you the sound of the breeze rustling the leaves in the trees. You lie for a while, enjoying the warmth of the sun, the gentle breeze and the sounds of the beach.

After a little while you sit up, stretch yourself and look around you. The beach is completely deserted, the sand golden, the sky blue and there is not a cloud to be seen. Higher up the beach you see a line of palm trees waving gently in the breeze, the green of their leaves highlighting the blue of the sky. Over the water a few gulls circle and call to one another. Beneath your hands you feel the soft, warm sand. Against your skin you feel the warm sun and the gentle breeze. You stand up and begin to walk down the waterline. You feel calm and at peace with the world. As you walk you enjoy the warmth of the sun and the feel of the sand beneath your feet. The gentle breeze caresses you skin. You notice tiny shells in the sand and the foam that each departing wave leaves behind sinks gently into the sand. Your steps take you into the edge of the water which is cooling on your feet, although still warm enough to be comfortable. The fresh sea air smells good and you fill your lungs, feeling the tranquillity and calm of the air and the sea. You walk further into the waves until they are lapping at your knees. As you gaze into the water around your legs, you notice the beautiful colours of the shells in the sand and the way the sunlight highlights first one colour, then another. In the water, tiny, brightly coloured fishes dart away from your approach. You continue walking, knee deep in the water, along the edge of the beach. The warm sunlight filling you with health and a sense of well-being. You are calm and relaxed, knowing that no harm can come to you.

As you gaze out across the waves you see larger fishes jumping and dancing in the water. You stop still and concentrate on what you are seeing. As your eyes come into focus you realise that you are watching a school of dolphins playing in the water. They are joyful and playful. As you stand watching you realise that a few of them are coming closer. There are two, maybe three dolphins dancing and playing quite near to you. You can hear their chirrups and clicks as they talk to each other. One of them comes quite close and you can see the sunlight glistening on her wet skin, the water frothing as she frolics. Realising they mean you no harm you wade deeper into the clear water until it reaches your waist. The dolphin swims slowly up to you, until you can reach out and touch her. She feels smooth and warm to the touch, as she rolls back in the water you stroke her chin and belly and the trust she shows in you brings you feelings of greater confidence. The sun is still warm above you and the sand is only a few steps away, knowing you can move away whenever you wish, you decide to stay awhile with the dolphins. The confidence of the one dolphin brings the other two nearer, and soon they are swimming and playing near enough for you to touch.

If you wish, you can enter the water, play with them and hold their backs whilst they swim. If you prefer you can remain standing waist deep whilst they frolic and brush gently past you. Whichever you decide to do you will feel calm and relaxed and totally safe. (long pause . . .)

After some time the dolphins begin to drift away, they call to you with their cheerful clicks and cries. You become aware once more of the warmth of the sun and the refreshing cool of the water. You wade slowly through the water back to the beach. Once again you enjoy the feeling of the sand beneath your feet and the warm light breeze against your skin. Already you are being dried by the sun and the air. Once again the only sounds are the lapping of the waves and the cries of the gulls. You make your way to the edge of the sand and lie down in the shade of a tree. You feel the warm sand supporting your body, the gentle breeze and the warm sun caressing your skin. You breath deeply, savouring the fresh sea air. You feel relaxed and at peace with the world. Your body feels renewed by the golden sunlight. Your mind and spirit feel healed by the trust of the animals you met in the water. You close your eyes and rest, safe in the arms of the world around you. You breath deeply, in through your nose to the count of four, hold

for the count of four, breathe out through you mouth to the count of four.
(Finish with the closing portion of the Relaxation Technique.)

PATHWORKING TO MEET THE GOD PAN:
(A deepening of the relaxation has been included in the middle of this Pathworking. Enclosed by the symbols * it may be omitted if preferred. Alternatively it may be inserted into other Pathworkings and Meditations, at any suitable point, or used with the Relaxation Technique as a simple relaxation. You will also notice that the participants are allowed to choose whether to follow the path or wait for the others. This allows those who have started the journey, but who are honest enough to know they are not ready to face Pan, the option.)

You are walking slowly through open meadows. The sun above is warm and the meadow grass is waving gently in the breeze. It is the height of summer and lazy butterflies flit from flower to flower. You can smell the sweet scents of summer, the meadow grass, the warm earth, the summer flowers. You can hear the crickets whispering in the tall grasses. You are calm and relaxed and know nothing and no-one can harm you.

You stroll gently on, savouring the heat of the summer sun and the clear blue sky. This is one of the lazy days of summer. A time without time, when all the anxieties and cares of everyday life seem to drift away from you leaving only a warm contented peace.

Ahead of you, you see a forest. Large ancient trees offering coolness from the heat of the sun. You let your steps take you towards the trees. As you come to the forest's edge you can sense the feeling of age and permanence that these ancient trees give out. A deep feeling of peace and security which washes over you and through you.

You step into the forest. It is cooler and darker under the canopy of the trees. The sunlight filtering through the treetops throws a greenish light over everything. Now that you are closer you can see that the trees are indeed very old. This is one of the ancient forests which used to cover our land. It is a place of magic and enchantment.

The ground beneath your feet is soft with the fallen leaves of many seasons, and your steps make no sound. You walk slowly onwards into the magical forest. As you go you take time to notice your surroundings. There are tall wide oaks, the tree of strength; twining around their trunks is ancient ivy, symbol of endurance, and high in their boughs the sacred mistletoe. You see graceful ash trees, tall and elegant reaching to the sky. There are protective rowans, the healing tree, covered with red berries. Here and there you see dark hollies, with their white flowers, harbinger of the fruit of winter and a symbol of the green man. All around you are the trees and plants of ancient times and you know that his place has been protected and nurtured for its sacred plants.

As you walk on deeper into the trees your sense of calm and relaxation deepens. The deeper into the forest you go the further you go from the mundane world and the more you let go of your worries and concerns. This is a place apart from the world. Here time has stopped and ceased to be. Not a sound disturbs the stillness and the dark green filtered light makes this a world of enchantments and magic.

Gradually the ground slopes downwards and the trees and shrubs become denser. Threading your way between the trunks you continue onwards. Here and there are the fallen boughs of trees who are continuing their cycle of life and death. Returning to the earth that others may grow and flourish in their place. Some of these fallen boughs are covered with dark green moss, others are already rotting. And in the warm, damp, darkness you can smell the scents of wood and earth, of life and of death and of rebirth.

Soon you reach a part of the forest more overgrown than the rest. Here the ground is covered with dense undergrowth, new life growing out the fallen trees and the deep carpet of leaves. Here you decide to rest and you settle yourself down leaning against the trunk of a tree.

As you close your eyes you can feel the spirit of the forest folding itself around you, protecting you.

* A word comes into your mind, that word is Relaxation. The essence of Relaxation is within you and all around you. You can feel the Relaxation behind every noise you hear. Relaxation is entering you with every breath you take. Relaxation that increases your feeling of well being and sense of security, that takes you deeper into yourself until you can hear only my voice. As the word Relaxation fades from your mind, its essence remains deep within you. Relaxation will be there for you at any time you need it.

A new word enters your mind. That word is Healing. Healing is within you and all around you. Healing is underlying every thought you have and entering you with every breath you take. Healing soothes you and washes away all the stresses of life. Healing that deepens your relaxation and allows your inner self to become one and strengthen you. The word Healing fades from your mind but its essence remains deep within you and will be there whenever you need it.

Healing is replaced by Love. Love is within you and all around you. You can feel the spirit of Love underlying every thought. Love enters you with every breath you take. Love that takes you deeper still into yourself where you are aware only of what I say and of the forest around you. Love which continues to heal your heart, your mind and your body. The essence of Love becomes a part of you, deep within you. The word Love fades from your mind, but it's essence remains deep within you. Love will be inside you and you can reach for it any time you need it.

The essence of Relaxation, together with the essence of Healing, joins the essence of Love deep inside of you to produce Wholeness. Wholeness that takes you deeper into relaxation and allows your inner self to take you further on the journey with my voice. A Wholeness that will be a part of you always and will be there whenever you need it. *

Still leaning against the tree in the forest, you open your eyes and find that the day has passed and it is now dusk, the twilight time. Here deep within the trees, the bright sunlight has faded and it is half-lit and mysterious. The trees cast shadows which shift and change in the half light. The forest is still friendly but in a darker and quieter way.

As your eyes adjust to the twilight you become aware of a strange figure watching you from a short distance away. He has dark curly hair, and looking closer you can see two small horns just peeking out from the curls. He is seated on a log, and resting one of his feet on the wood beside him, his fur covered legs end in hooves. In his hands he holds a set of musical pipes. His face is mischievous and merry as he regards you. As he takes up the pipes and starts to play you realise you are in the presence of Pan, ancient God of the forest.

The music he plays is captivating and exciting, and as the notes wash over you, you feel them penetrate into your inner being. They heal and soothe, calm and relax you whilst making you feel light-hearted and happy. You sit awhile and listen. (pause . . .)

He rises to his feet and beckons you to follow him. You may choose to do so or you may remain where you are sitting and rejoin the journey later.

If you choose to follow Pan do so now. He leads you deeper into the woods to where there is a broad open space filled with music and laughter. Here there are many strange beings, wood nymphs, elves, gnomes and others. There are also other people like yourself, all are dancing around a fire in the centre of the grove. All are dancing to the music of Pan. They invite you to join in their celebrations, so you join the dance. (pause . . .)

After a while you leave the dance and go to where Pan is playing the pipes. He beckons you closer and bids you sit by his side. In a hollow in the wood between you is a small dark pool. He tells you that you may look once into the pool but that you must choose whether to see into the past, the present or the future, or you may choose not to look at all. Make your choice now. (pause . . .) If you choose to look into the water do so now, watch the images carefully to remember all you can (pause . . .).

When you have finished gazing into the waters you look up. All around you is still and quiet once more. Pan and the festive dancers have gone. The fire has died down and you are alone sitting against the trunk of the tree where you first sat down.

If you chose not to follow Pan you will rejoin the journey now.

Night has fallen and the forest has come alive with the sounds of night animals going about their business. Guided by the moon you retrace your steps back out of the forest. Noticing the way that moonlight changes everything around you.

As you reach the forest's edge you pause, and in the distance you seem to hear the pipes of Pan and the sound of a gentle chuckle.

You continue out of the forest and as you walk you remember all the sights and events that took place. As you walk through the fields the images start to fade and you become aware again of the sound of my voice, the floor beneath you supporting you, the weight of your limbs on the floor and the room you are now in.

(Finish with the closing portion of the Relaxation Technique.)

There are many books available which give Pathworkings and Guided Meditations suitable for group use. Some are Wiccan oriented others are more general. Alternatively, you can write your own. If you are in a working group it is a good idea to get everyone to have a go, as it's a talent that may surprise them and you. This applies to readers too, some people have the ability naturally, others may have to develop it.

The guidelines for writing and running Pathworkings are as follows:

The story should have a beginning a middle and an end. It should also flow, no sudden surprises. Ease them gently from relaxation into the substance of the story.

Try to ensure that there is sufficient description to keep the participants occupied. The more you describe the easier it is for them to get into the setting.

Avoid threatening settings and circumstances, for a Pathworking to work people must feel safe.

With 'heavier' Pathworkings check your seasonal, moon and planetary influences. For example you would not want to do the Pathworking to Pan at Samhain, it might, however, be very interesting at Beltane!

Never try to include subliminal suggestions, even if a group member asks for help in, say, giving up smoking, resist the temptation. Unless you are a qualified hypnotherapist you may do more harm than good.

Although this is a group event, respect the wishes and feelings of the individuals. If one person is, say, afraid of heights, warn them in advance, so they may choose not to take part, perhaps they would like to be reader this time.

Don't force people to share their experiences with the group, some of the things seen and heard on a Pathworking can be very personal. Get them to discuss this with the High Priestess, High Priest or team leader at a later date.

Participants should be encouraged to interpret their own experiences — their first thoughts or instincts are more likely to be right.

Pathworkings must be written up, in a Book of Shadows if you have one, or in a dream diary. It is often sometime after the event that the meaning becomes clear, and it is not easy to remember all the detail weeks or months later.

The authors regularly write Pathworkings for their Coven and are happy to help enquirers. They can also supply recorded Pathworkings and Meditations on cassette, those interested can contact them on the internet at www.pyewacket.demon.co.uk.

COVENS AND INITIATIONS

The Coven is the family group of the Witches. Coven members celebrate together, work together and should be prepared to help one another. Their ties should be as strong as that of blood relationship, family or clan. The Coven may follow a collective tradition (e.g. Celtic, Nordic etc.), or may work with mixed traditions, in which case Coven members select and follow their own path(s). Coven members will also work on their own, in fact they are expected to.

The High Priestess and High Priest are like the parents of the family. They are there to guide and advise, answer questions and form the individuals into a cohesive group. It is worth noting, that whilst more knowledgeable and experienced, the High Priestess and High Priest are still human. They are not there to do all the work! They command respect because they earn it.

Witches do not recruit, unlike other religions, as a result anyone who wants to join the Coven must ask. Those wishing to join the Coven will be examined by the High Priestess and/or High Priest in order to be sure that their motives are sincere, and to ensure that they will fit in with the other Coven members. In most cases there is usually a lengthy period between first approaching a Coven and being accepted. This is as it should be, the Craft is a serious religion to those who have chosen it as their path, not something to be taken lightly. There is still a lot of prejudice and misunderstanding around, the High Priestess and High Priest also have a duty to existing Coven members. Some Covens will accept any number of entrants, others prefer to limit numbers. Being turned down by a Coven is not necessarily a reflection on the individual as it may be governed by outside constraints.

Those who join a Coven are expected to attend the Sabbats and to participate in those celebrations and workings, and, whenever possible, to do likewise with the Esbats (Full Moons). This is not to say that any old excuse will do, a certain level of commitment is expected! They may or may not be invited to join in other rituals or workings. It is not necessary to become initiated to join the Coven, it is however necessary to observe the confidentiality of the group members, before, during and (where applicable) after being a member of the Coven. This is often covered by a Coven Oath. The Oath is taken before the rest of the Coven and is usually administered at the first Closed working that a person attends. The Oath is a promise made by the individual on 'their honour', it contains no threats or repercussions. It is considered that a person who fails to uphold this, or any other promise, is answerable to their own conscience and to the Goddess and the God.

Initiation means to begin. In the Craft, Initiation is a promise made by the individual to his or her Goddess(es) and God(s). The Coven is there to assist and facilitate that promise. There are other elements to Initiation oaths but these can be gone into in depth at the proper time.

No-one is forced into Initiation, it is an individual's choice. It is up to an individual to ask for Initiation. It is the responsibility of the High Priestess and/or High Priest to judge whether or not that person is ready.

In the Gardnerian and Alexandrian paths Initiation consists of three stages; 1st, 2nd and 3rd Degree. Some other traditions have no levels, some have up to eight. The stages in Gardnerian and Alexandrian are as follows:

1st Degree is the beginning and represents the individual's decision that this is the right path for them and their commitment to the Craft. Traditionally, 1st Degree Initiation occurs at the end of 1 year and 1 day of preparation and training. Nowadays this varies, and could take place after a few months or many years.

2nd Degree, acknowledges that the person is now ready to pass on their knowledge of the Craft, with all the responsibilities that this entails.

3rd Degree, often taken concurrently with 2nd, acknowledges that the person is now ready and able, to form and run an autonomous Coven.

The style of Initiation varies from Coven to Coven. Most Covens initiate skyclad, although some are prepared to do otherwise. Those who are not already initiated may not, in some Covens, be allowed to observe initiations or to know who has and who has not been initiated.

Those who are already initiated elsewhere but who wish to join the Coven are often required to undergo Initiation into that specific Coven. This is usually done to help to bond the Coven members.

Initiation may, or may not, include the taking of a Witch name. This is a name chosen by the initiate to mark the change in their life and can be the name of a deity, hero or heroine, plant, animal or place of special significance to the initiate. The Witch name then becomes the name under which the Witch is known to the Coven within the closed circle. Where a Witch name is taken it is usually done so at Second Degree. Originally, Witch names were used to conceal the identity of Coven members, making it impossible for their fellows to give them away, even under torture. The Rite of naming can also be undergone at other times.

Self Initiation can also be performed. This can be guided by a High Priestess and/or High Priest if desired and agreed upon.

There are no sacrificial virgins involved in Coven membership or in Initiation!!! Sexual intercourse will be token or more often symbolic. Whilst the Craft is open in its enjoyment of the physical pleasures of life (hence all the feasting), it is not the place for the prurient or sensation seekers.

Should an individual, initiated or otherwise, chose to leave the Coven, this is their decision, and whilst this is usually a cause of sadness, no threats or coercion will be used to try to prevent it.

If a member of the Coven does not abide by the rules of the Coven, is disruptive, brings the Craft into disrepute, or does not show the required level of commitment to the Craft, they may be asked to leave. In most cases, they may not ask for re-admission to that, or any other Coven, for a year and a day. The world of Witches is small and close knit, the name of a banished person, together with their misdeeds, will be known to almost every other Coven within a few days, or weeks, of such an event.

One other event which should be mentioned is the disbanding of a Coven. This, rather extreme decision, may have to be taken in cases where one, or more, of the Coven members proves incapable of keeping the necessary silence. It is a sad fact of life that, to a few, joining a Coven is simply another social event which they feel the urge to share with all and sundry. Should you find yourself in a disbanded Coven, and you are certain that you are not the cause, it is often worth approaching the High Priestess or High Priest, after a suitable interval, to ask whether there is any chance of the Coven reforming.

IN CONCLUSION

I am often asked what it takes to become a Witch and my answer is that I often think of the Craft as containing three parts; the Religion, the Rituals and the Magic. If a person considers that the beliefs of a Witch are their beliefs then that person can call themselves a Witch, whether they have found a Coven or prefer to work on their own. To gain an understanding of the Rituals of the Craft they need to have followed a full cycle of the Wheel of the Year, and to have celebrated all the Sabbats and Esbats that it contains. To be able to perform the magic however, is a journey which lasts a lifetime. It is necessary to understand and embrace not only the Elements of Air, Fire, Water and Earth but also the fifth element, that of Spirit, and to understand their relationship to the Divine. Once these three parts have been combined then a person has truly begun to walk the path of the Witch.

In the Craft we are each our own Priest or Priestess, and there is no formal hierarchy outside of that which exists within each Coven. Hence there is no formal 'training system'. In fact the Craft cannot be taught by one person to another, an experienced Witch may act as guide or mentor, but it is the individual's efforts, supported by the Goddess and the God, which enables them to grow and learn within the Craft. Additionally, the Craft itself is not static, it is a living and growing belief system and so each of us who follow the path will never cease learning and growing. The personal responsibility and development which we embrace as part of our beliefs link us to a constant journey of exploration and discovery, not just of the Craft but also of ourselves and our place within it.

Just as no one person can teach another the Craft so no one book can ever be a complete guide to the Craft. There are a great many excellent books available today on the Craft the following is a list of some which may be useful. This might be in a general way, or because they specialise in a particular area which is too complex to be covered in an all round text. Many of these books are intended to be used as reference, rather than to be read as literature. If a book is not listed here it does not mean it is not a valuable work, nor is it intended as a slight to the author. Equally, not every book here will suit every reader, as each has his or her requirements in terms of content, and preferences when it comes to style. If you find yourself reading something you find tedious or 'heavy going', do not feel that you have a problem, it may simply be that you and that work are not compatible. You may find some of these books are out of print, however, it should be possible with perseverance to locate them through the library system.

FURTHER READING:

- Kate West. *Pagan Rites of Passage,* Mandrake Press Ltd., 1997. A series of booklets giving information and rituals for the Rites of Passage of Handfasting, Naming and Withdrawal.

- Kate West. *The Real Witches' Handbook,* Harper Collins 2000. Real Witchcraft for real people with real lives, this book shows how to practise the Craft in a way sensitive to those around you.

- Kate West. *The Real Witches' Kitchen,* Harper Collins 2002. Oils, lotions and ointments for Magic and to relieve and heal. Soaps and bathing distillations for Circle and Magical work. Magical incenses, candles and sachets to give or to keep. Food and drink to celebrate the Sabbats, for personal wellbeing and to share with friends.

- Kate West. *A Spell in your Pocket,* Harper Collins 2002. A handy pocket-sized gift book for the Witch on the move.

- Kate West. *The Real Witches' Coven,* Harper Collins 2003. A complete guide to forming and running a Coven, with real and humorous anecdotes from the author. Rituals of Initiation, the Sabbats and to mark the phases of the Moon.

- Kate West. *The Real Witches' Book of Spells and Rituals,* Harper Collins, June 2003. A comprehensive grimoire with: Rituals for the Sabbats, Esbats and other phases of the Moon. Rites of Passage, of healing, growth and development. Spells for use in all areas of living in today's world.

GENERAL BOOKS ON THE CRAFT

- J W Baker, *The Alex Sanders Lectures*, Magickal Childe, 1984. A perspective on Alexandrian Witchcraft.
- Rae Beth, *Hedgewitch*, Hale, 1990. Solitary Witchcraft, written as a series of letters to newcomers.
- Janice Broch and Veronica MacLer, *Seasonal Dance*, Weiser 1993. New ideas for the Sabbats.
- Janet and Stewart Farrar, *A Witches Bible* (formerly *The Witches' Way* and *Eight Sabbats for Witches*). Phoenix 1996. Alexandrian Craft as it is practised.
- Gerald Gardner, *The Meaning of Witchcraft*, Rider & Co., 1959; reissued by Mandrake Press Ltd., 2000. Gardnerian Witchcraft.
- Pattalee Glass-Koentop, *Year of Moons, Season of Trees*, Llewellyn, 1991. Information on the Tree calendar and ideas to incorporate at the Full Moons.
- Paddy Slade, *Natural Magic*, Hamlyn, n.d. A perspective on Traditional Witchcraft.
- Doreen Valiente, *ABC of Witchcraft*, Hale, 1973. Gardnerian Craft written in 'dictionary' form.
- Doreen Valiente, *The Charge of the Goddess*, Hexagon Hoopix, 2000. A collection of the poetry and thoughts from the 'Mother of Modern Witchcraft'. Compiled and published after her death, this work gives a unique insight into the development of the modern Craft.

BOOKS ON PARTICULAR ASPECTS OF THE CRAFT

- Anne Llewellyn Barstow, *Witchcraze*, Harper Collins, 1995. Detailed history of the persecution of Witches.
- Jean Shinola Bolen, *Goddesses in Everywoman*, Harper Collins, 1985. A guide to finding the Goddess within, and a wealth of tales about the aspects of the Goddess.

- Scott Cunningham, *Cunningham's Encyclopaedia of Magical Herbs*, Llewellyn, 1985. Magical uses, and tales surrounding most common herbs.
- Scott Cunningham, *Cunningham's Encyclopaedia of Crystal, Gem and Metal Magic,* Llewellyn, 1988. Magical properties of most gemstones available today.
- Scott Cunningham, *The Complete Book of Oils, Incenses and Brews,* Llewellyn, 1989. Magical preparation and use of oils, incenses and other mixtures.
- Janet and Stewart Farrar, *The Witches' Goddess*, Hale, 1987. Examination of some of the more common Goddesses.
- Janet and Stewart Farrar, *The Witches' God*, Hale, 1989. Examination of some of the more common Gods.
- Marian Green, *A Calendar of Festivals, Element Books, 1991.* Descriptions of festivals, not just Pagan or Wiccan, around the year with practical things to do, make and cook.
- Mrs M Grieve, *A Modern Herbal,* Jonathan Cape, 1931; reissued Tiger, 1992. A detailed reference for the serious herbalist; identification, preparation and use of herbs, ancient and modern. Also available on the Internet at *http://www.botanical.com/botanical/mgmh/mgmh.html.*
- Paul Katzeff, *Moon Madness*, Citadel, 1981. A study of the effects of the Moon and many of the legends and mythology associated with it. Not an easy read, but well worth the effort.
- Patricia Monaghan, *The Book of Goddesses and Heroines*, Llewellyn, 1981. A definitive guide to major and minor Goddesses from around the world.
- Jeffrey B Russell, *A History of Witchcraft*, Thames & Hudson, 1983. A factual history of the Craft.
- Egerton Sykes, *Who's Who Non-Classical Mythology*, Oxford University Press, 1993. A dictionary of Gods and Goddesses.
- Bill Whitcomb, *The Magician's Companion,* Llewellyn, 1993. Possibly the 'ultimate' reference work for correspondences and symbols.

OTHER PUBLICATIONS WHICH MAY BE OF INTEREST

- Children of Artemis, *Witchcraft and Wicca*, top quality bi-annual magazine written by Witches for Witches. Articles, poetry, rituals, spells, art, crafts and events, and much more.

- Clarissa Pinkola Estes, *Women who Run With the Wolves*, Rider 1993. This is not a book on the Craft. However, it discusses the hidden meanings behind many tales and fables, and as such it opens the mind to the interpretation of stories which may have suffered through time and translation. Whilst this 'self-help' book is written for women it does have relevance for both genders.

- Terry Pratchett, *Witches' Abroad, Wyrd Sisters, Masquerade, Lords and Ladies, etc*. Corgi Books. Recommended for their powers of relaxation and the regeneration of a sense of humour after a hard day. They are pure fiction and give a humorous perspective on the world of fictitious (?) Witches!

POINTS OF CONTACT

The following organisations facilitate contact, or provide information on Witchcraft and Paganism. Please always enclose a stamped addressed envelope, and remember that some of these organisations may not allow membership to people under the age of 18 years.

- *The Children of Artemis* – Initiated Witches who seek to find reputable training Covens for genuine seekers. Their magazine *Witchcraft and Wicca* is almost certainly the best on the Craft today. BM Box Artemis, London WC1N 3XX. http://www.witchcraft.org <contact@witchcraft.org>

- *ASLaN* – Information on the care and preservation of Sacred

Sites all over Britain. http://www.symbolstone.org/archaeology/aslan. <andy.norfolk@connectfree.co.uk>

- *The Witches' Voice* — One of the best American sources of information about the Craft. P.O. Box 4924, Clearwater, Florida 33758-4924, USA. http://www.witchvox.com

- *Inform* — Totally independent and not aligned to any religious organisation or group. Their primary aim is to help people by providing them with accurate, objective and up-to-date information on new religious movements, alternative religions, unfamiliar belief systems and 'cults'. Houghton Street, London WC2A 2AE. 020 7955 7654

MANDRAGORA CATALOGUES
for all your Kate West and Wiccan books

BLUE BOOK

The *Blue Book* is our 196 page perfect bound *Stock* catalogue of the 4250+ items we keep in stock, this catalogue includes the following:
- Complete *Mandrake Press* catalogue with descriptions of all the titles from *I-H-O Books*, *First Impressions* and *Pentacle Enterprises*, including authors such as Gerald Gardner, Austin Osman Spare, Frederick Carter and Keith Morgan.
- Complete illustrated catalogue of the 1250+ *Indio Products* including Candles, Incenses, Jewellery, Oils, Soaps, Bath Products, Religious Items and much more. Mandragora is the sole distributor in the UK of *Indio Products Inc.*, the world's most complete manufacturer of Spiritual, Religious and New Age Items.
- Complete illustrated *Eastgate Resource* catalogue of silver, pewter and brass jewellery collections, including Viking, Celtic, Mediaeval, Ethnic, Magical and Fantasy ranges, plus New Age cards and magical gifts.
- Complete *Llewellyn* subject catalogue with descriptions of their 500+ titles on Astrology; Feng Shui; The Golden Dawn; Health and Healing; Magic, Spells and Rituals; Paganism; Reiki; Tarot Books, Deck and Kits; Wicca and Witchcraft; and much more. *Llewellyn* is America's oldest publisher of books on New Age and Occult Sciences.
- Complete *Thorsons–Element* subject catalogue with descriptions of their 480+ titles. *Thorsons–Element* (part of the *HarperCollins* publishing group) is the UK's leading publisher of mind, body and spirit titles, covering a diverse range of subjects including alternative health, natural therapies, ancient wisdom and modern-day spirituality, relationships and sex, and personal development books.
- Descriptions of new and forthcoming titles from such publishers as *Capall Bann, Red Wheel–Weiser, Piatkus, Foulsham, Rider, David and Charles*, etc., etc.
- Complete stock items subject catalogue made up of 72 subjects covering over 2790 books, kits, and decks.

YELLOW BOOK

A *Personal Import Service* for Mandragora customers. The *Yellow Book* is compiled from USA Distributors' lists and is our 186 page *Special Order* catalogue of over 13,500 products in 290+ subject categories. All products ordered from this catalogue will be imported especially for *you*.

To receive the *Blue Book* and *Yellow Book* send £1.95 to
MANDRAGORA, ESSEX HOUSE, THAME, OX9 3LS. ENGLAND
(plus £2.50 post and packing — UK and Europe only)

BUY ON-LINE AT
www.mandrake-press.com

OUR WEBSITE INCLUDES THE FOLLOWING FEATURES:

Secure on-line ordering system
Complete listings of all our stock items
Full search capability
Exclusive Web only special offers and sales